THE BACCHAE OF EURIPIDES

D0873098

THE BACCHAE
OF
EURIPIDES

Translated with an introduction and commentary by

G. S. KIRK

*Regius Professor of Greek in the University
of Cambridge, and Fellow of Trinity College*

CAMBRIDGE UNIVERSITY PRESS

Cambridge

London   New York   Melbourne

Published by the Syndics of the Cambridge University Press
The Pitt Building, Trumpington Street, Cambridge CB2 1RP
Bentley House, 200 Euston Road, London NW1 2DB
32 East 57th Street, New York, NY 10022, USA
296 Beaconsfield Parade, Middle Park, Melbourne 3206, Australia

First published by Prentice-Hall in their Greek Drama Series in 1970
First published by the Cambridge University Press 1979

Printed in the United States of America by
Vail-Ballou Press, Inc.

Library of Congress Cataloguing in Publication Data

Euripides.

The Bacchae of Euripides.

Reprint of the 1970 ed. published by Prentice-Hall,
Englewood Cliffs, N.J., in series: Prentice-Hall
Greek drama series.

Bibliography: p.

I. Kirk, Geoffrey Stephen. II. Title.

PA3975.B2K5   1979   882'.01   78-31827
ISBN 0 521 22675 9 hard covers
ISBN 0 521 29613 7 paperback

CONTENTS

TRANSLATOR'S PREFACE

The commentator on *The Bacchae* has two great advantages: a marvellous play and an outstanding modern edition of it. E. R. Dodds' work is primarily directed to the student of the play in Greek. My aim is different: I am primarily trying to provide the Greekless reader with an accurate line-by-line translation and an untechnical but analytical commentary. Yet there are few points at which I have not been helped by Dodds' *Bacchae*, and it is to this book (2nd ed., Oxford 1960) that I refer any reader who looks for more specialized guidance. At the same time I have tried to see the play and its problems in an independent way, and, even on detailed matters of Greek which are not mentioned in the commentary, I have made up my mind at each point, conscious that classical scholars are so thorough that they might show interest in a book not designed for them. In a few cases, indeed, I have given a short and very simplified account of linguistic or textual problems, mainly to show what kind of effect they have on the meaning of the play as a whole. Much of the commentary is necessarily devoted to the choral odes (where the line-numbering, incidentally, occasionally looks curious, but for valid textual and historical reasons). Where the narrative is self-explanatory and quite clear in translation, as it often is, I have tried to keep quiet.

Other recent contributions to the text and interpretation of the play have been useful in varying degrees. I have followed W. J. Verdenius (*Mnemosyne* 15, 1962, 337 ff.) in about a third of the cases where he disagrees with or supplements Dodds, and have been helped by Mme J. Roux's edition (*Euripide, les Bacchantes*, 2 vols., Paris 1970–2) at three important points; by C. W. Willink's article (*Classical Quarterly*, N.S. 16, 1966, 27 ff. and 220 ff.), as it happens, relatively seldom.

My more personal debts are sixfold: to the lamented Alan Ker, who died before he could improve more than the first 150 lines of the translation; to Hugh Lloyd-Jones, who made available to me the draft of his enlightening section on the Dionysus-plays of Aeschylus; to Mrs Marylin Whitfield, who read the translation and commentary and made·many valuable criticisms; to my Yale colleagues Eric Havelock and Adam Parry, whose careful scrutiny of what I had written exceeded normal editorial attentions and was almost, one might say, an education in itself; and to Dr James Diggle, who is responsible for a number of further corrections and improvements in this latest version.

GEOFFREY S. KIRK

INTRODUCTION

The Bacchae was written at the end of Euripides' life and was not produced in Athens until 405 B.C., a year or so after he died. It, and the plays produced with it (of which only the very different *Iphigeneia at Aulis* survives), won the first prize that had usually eluded Euripides—which is not surprising, for *The Bacchae* is the most perfect of all his works, in the class of Aeschylus' *Agamemnon* and Sophocles' *Oedipus the King*. It is almost unbelievable that a play so vigorous, so carefully planned, and so beautifully written should be the work of a man well over seventy. Could he perhaps have drafted it earlier and only brought it to its final form when, in the last two years of his life, he had abandoned Athens for the new-world comforts of the court of King Archelaus of Macedon? Nothing we know of the ideals and methods of writers in Greece makes this probable, and the treatment of the iambic metre marks the detailed composition of the play as late. Yet for its form and conception the author was certainly looking back into his own literary past. Certain qualities of *The Bacchae* remind one strongly of his *Hippolytus*, produced many years before in 428 B.C.: the similarity of the roles of Dionysus and Aphrodite, and above all the underlying theme of the cost of resisting those gods who reside in human nature itself, whether they demand expression in sexual passion or in the ecstasies of an extraordinary religion.

1

A deliberate reversion to the past is indicated, too, by the formal structure of *The Bacchae*. The Chorus, which had been relatively unimportant in most of the later plays of Sophocles and Euripides, here becomes once again a major factor. The Lydian women who have followed their apparently human leader to Thebes are a stronger element in the drama—because they are more directly concerned in its outcome and are involved in fewer paradoxes of inaction—than almost any other chorus we know. The substitution of lyric solos for choral odes, progressively undertaken by Euripides in the last twenty years of his life, is here abandoned. In its ode of entry the Chorus expresses the feelings and beliefs of Dionysus' true followers; and then, in carefully spaced and finely made songs, in simple rhythms and a language that is often Aeschylean, it passes from professions of moderation and peace to the demand for vengeance on Pentheus, a movement that provides a kind of moral and emotional metronome of the entire action.

The poet was seeking not only a classical form from the past but also a classical subject. Of his own plays several seem to have touched on ecstatic forms of religion; and one of them, the lost *Cretans*, was a play of comparative youth. In its one substantial fragment we hear of the initiates of Idaean Zeus, of the thunder of night-wandering Zagreus (a form of Dionysus), of feasts of raw flesh, of Couretes and bacchants, of the wearing of white garments, and of the avoidance of contact with birth, death, and ordinary animal food (frag. 472 Nauck[2]). Elements of Dionysiac worship are mixed with other similar cult practices in a syncretistic manner that reminds one strongly of verses 120–34 of *The Bacchae*. In spite of this evidently long-standing interest, Euripides seems to have devoted no other play to a wholly Dionysiac subject. Yet many in his audience must have been familiar with such plays. Aeschylus, in particular, had written two tetralogies on Dionysiac themes. One told the story of Lycurgus, a Thracian Pentheus who also tried to resist the god and also suffered for it. The other dealt with the Theban story, beginning with a complete play on Dionysus' birth (*Semele*), continuing, probably, with the maddening of the Theban women (*Xantriae*), following with a treatment of the opposition and death of Pentheus (*Pentheus*), and ending with a lighter affair, a so-called Satyr play,

2

The Nurses of Dionysus. Pentheus in particular must have had much in common with our play; but other themes connect *The Bacchae* also with the Lycurgus tetralogy, about which we happen to be a little better informed. The effeminate appearance of the god, his imprisonment and escape, and miracles in the palace—all these certainly occurred in that tetralogy; they may have been traditional even before that, and at least cannot have been novel to the audiences who saw them repeated in Euripides. Much of the story of *The Bacchae* strikes us as remarkable and unique, but much of it, most of it probably, was certainly not so then. Our view of Greek tragedy is almost one-dimensional. We see a few peaks towering above the mist and admire their beauty and splendid isolation; but audiences at the Great Dionysia, the yearly dramatic festival in Athens, knew a complete landscape of myth and tragedy; they saw how the high peaks were connected with each other and with a whole mass of lower eminences of which we are substantially ignorant.

Why did Euripides choose to revive the well-known theme of Dionysus and his worship? In a sense he was merely completing his lifetime as a dramatist by writing about the god to whom tragedy was devoted and out of whose dithyrambic worship it had probably arisen. Beyond that, he was surely affected by the new aspect that the Dionysiac cults must have assumed in the light of the foreign ecstatic religions of Bendis, Cybele, Sabazius, Adonis, and Isis, which were introduced from Asia Minor and the Levant and swept through Piraeus and Athens during the frustrating and increasingly irrational years of the Peloponnesian War. Euripides' attitude to these new cults is a matter for speculation; but perhaps he now saw more clearly the connection between their kind of emotion and the emotions he had explored so penetratingly in *Medea* and *Hippolytus* two decades before. There are, of course, other factors. The story of Pentheus was plainly a dramatic one and would gain heavily from the new standards of realism and shock that Euripides was prepared to apply and his audiences conditioned to accept. In its different kinds of conflict it provided ideal material for the rhetorical exchanges of which Euripides was a master. Less obviously, he may have seen the opportunity for a fresh kind of originality, nothing to do with new ways of singing or new and startling characters, but one that depended on the contrast between a severe and archaistic form and a wild, uninhibited subject.

What can be objectively determined about the religion of Dionysus? Evidence is scarce for the period before Euripides, and afterwards it proliferates almost uncontrollably. Partly this seems to reflect the nature of Dionysus himself—his increasing multiformity and the way in which he became attached, in one of his aspects or another, to different kinds of cult. First there is Dionysus the god of ecstatic female worshippers, whose cult is resisted, especially in the north. The one important reference in Homer (who as a whole pays little attention to this god) concerns his clash with Lycurgus in Thrace (*Iliad* 6. 130–37). Andromache rushes like a maenad—literally, a madwoman—at *Iliad* 22. 460, and the *Hymn to Demeter*, composed probably in the late seventh century B.C., expands the image, in verse 386, to a maenad darting on a forested mountain—quite definitely a Dionysiac sort of maenad. Partly coinciding with this ecstatic form of the god is the Dionysus who is associated with the fertility and wildness of rampant nature, with ivy and forest trees and the power and fertility of animals and the wild life of the mountains: so also in *The Bacchae* and in Pindar, though not in the early epic. In both of these overlapping aspects Dionysus has something in common with the Thracian Orpheus. (Yet it is possible that in one version of his myth Orpheus became an opponent of Dionysus and that his rending by the Bassarids, who were followers of the god, was described in the play of that name from Aeschylus' Lycurgus group.)

The second aspect in turn overlaps a third: Dionysus as god of the vine and its husbandry, of the opening of the new wine in springtime, and of all festivals celebrated with gaiety and drinking. It appears that this was not his original function but perhaps a special application of his fertility associations—for the vine, like ivy, proliferates wildly—which then became dominant in many places, as it certainly did in Attica. Dionysus is already god of the joy of wine in Hesiod (although Homer ignores this aspect), and wine is among his benefits to men in *The Bacchae*. Yet Euripides is careful not to exaggerate the part wine must have played from comparatively early times in the celebrations of bacchants. Indeed in the series of vase

4

paintings of bacchants from the sixth century B.C. onward the women are never shown drunk themselves, although they are sometimes accompanied by Satyrs, half-animal followers of the god who are characterized by drunkenness, gaiety, and lechery. At any rate, wine, as well as water, milk, and honey, flows miraculously from the earth in *The Bacchae* (704–11), and even Euripides does not try to exclude it entirely from the cult of the mountain dancers.

Long before the sixth century B.C., Dionysus must have been established in the old Ionic and Attic festival of the Anthesteria, which, as well as being a celebration of the opening of the new wine, was a chthonic festival at which the spirits of the dead returned from inside the earth to visit for a short time the land of the living. Thus to the Athenian spectators of *The Bacchae* the contradictions that they saw represented in the character of Dionysus were already, in a slightly different form, part of a familiar tradition; for he is god of joy, peace, and festivity on the one hand, of terror and the dead on the other. These are two sides of fertility; for fertility comes from the earth, but the earth is the place where the dead go. In many rustic festivals, particularly in Attica, fertility takes on another aspect, and Dionysus was worshipped with models of the phallus. Heraclitus of Ephesus, the pre-Socratic philosopher, early in the fifth century B.C. spoke of the procession to Dionysus in which a hymn is sung to the sexual parts; but (he adds) this Dionysus, for whom people are maddened and "become Lenai," is the same as Hades the god of the underworld (frag. 15). Now Lenai are Attic versions of bacchants, and the Lenaia was the minor dramatic festival of Athens. Heraclitus brings together many different strands: the frenzied female devotees, the fertility and phallic aspect of the god, the relationship with the dead, even perhaps the origins of drama. This is a different picture from that of *The Bacchae*, where the association of the god with human fertility and sex is suppressed or is found only in the curiosity of Pentheus, and where the connection with Hades is seen only in the murderous proclivities of the hyperbacchants on Cithaeron and in the devouring of raw flesh sought by the true bacchants who compose the Chorus.

It may be doubted whether any integrated conception of the god in all these aspects was commonly held during the fifth century, when Dionysus was already firmly established at Delphi under the aegis of Apollo and at Eleusis under the aegis of Demeter. This is important, because it means that Euripides could select, that he did not have to represent the god in all his aspects. It follows that Pentheus' voyeurism, for example, may be a deliberate development by the playwright rather than a mere concession to the myth or its associated ritual (which is not to deny that the exclusion of men from women's rites is a traditional theme). One final aspect of Dionysus may be missing from the play for simple chronological reasons: his own death by being torn to pieces and devoured by the Titans, the generation of early gods displaced by Zeus. The story is assigned to Onomacritus, a half-legendary collector of oracles and the like at the end of the sixth century B.C., but there are no certain references to it until the third century B.C. After that it becomes extremely common, part of the sacred literature of Orphism, in which Dionysus now has an important place. That Dionysus himself suffered dismemberment or tearing-to-pieces, *sparagmos*, just like the goat, fawn, or bull that was his usual sacrificial victim in the ecstatic mountain dances, is an intriguing thought which could be highly relevant to the interpretation of our play. Yet the whole story has looked like a late development to many critics, and I am inclined to agree for reasons that do not belong here. At all events, by the Greco-Roman period there were local cults of Dionysus of the most diverse kind (not least as patron of actors, who were now established in elaborate guilds); his ecstatic aspect, surely one of his oldest, and probably original to the god who was first introduced from Asia Minor, is now relatively less important, though still maintained in biennial rallies in many different parts of the Greek world.

It is clear that Euripides selects; he gives a dramatic picture of one type of Dionysiac worship, although it is the oldest and the best known. Yet even this picture is likely to be highly imaginative in places. To what extent, it may be asked, did bands of women really run wild in the hills in the depths of winter, led by an imagined god or his human priest, falling on young animals and suckling them or tearing them to pieces? Tamer relics of these things were familiar in the Greco-Roman period—but that is no infallible index of what happened before Euripides' time, and indeed, plays like *The Bacchae* (or rather *The Bacchae* in particular, which was immensely popular in the postclassical era) may have done much to determine the details of these later cults. Yet it is certain that Euripides was not simply making everything up. It has been the custom since the first appearance of Erwin Rohde's *Psyche* to point to other examples of something resembling maenadism: to the dancing madness of medieval times, to Abyssinians and dervishes and Kwakiutl Indians who match many of the feats described by Euripides, the balancing, the falling to the ground, the unpleasant fascination of eating raw flesh. The parallels are persuasive up to a point, and many of the characteristics of Dionysiac worship as Euripides describes it are likely to be founded on fact; but not all, and not exactly so founded, and that may be important. Fantasy and fiction can be proved in the case of the actual miracles (the wine and milk flowing from ground or rock, perhaps the earthquake that destroys part of the palace buildings at the god's command), and they obviously extended beyond the demonstrable cases—although even here it could be argued that what Euripides describes are illusions genuinely undergone by worshippers in a state of ecstasy.

E. R. Dodds in his rich commentary on the play, as well as in his book *The Greeks and the Irrational*,[1] has done much to show that many of the apparently fantastic details of ancient religious practice can be understood in the light of actual psychic phenomena. Yet I wonder whether he has not gone too far in implying that, because many of the details of Dionysus' worship seem to be based on observation, the general picture is accurate, not necessarily for the late fifth century but for the archaic past. Something akin to the mountain dancing described in the choral odes of *The Bacchae* must have taken place in Greece so as to become a familiar part of tradition, but whether it infected whole cities and large bodies of women is more doubtful. "Such a practice would have been alien to the spirit of seclusion which pervaded the life of womankind in Greece." These words, from the introduction to J. E. Sandys' late-nineteenth-century edition of the play, are rebutted by Dodds; but I wonder whether, despite their old-fashioned look, they do not contain an element of truth. It does seem incredible that in Greece, whatever happened in Asia Minor, women should have been allowed to run

---

[1] *Euripides, Bacchae*, Oxford, Clarendon Press, 2nd ed., 1960; *The Greeks and the Irrational*, Berkeley and Los Angeles, 1951.

wild as a regular practice in the manner described by the Chorus of *The Bacchae*. Of course this was precisely what Pentheus was trying to stop, and many critics have seen in this and other resistance myths a reflection of actual historical events; but the point is that in historical though not in dramatic terms he was likely to be ultimately successful. In this respect at least it appears that a dominant element in the myth—and one that may conceal certain other facts about the status of women—became the starting point for fantastic elaborations, mainly of a literary kind.

If Euripides' picture of the worship of Dionysus is an impressionistic and fantastic one, based on disparate and selective elements both of the literary and of the religious tradition, it may still be asked what his own attitude was. Did he intend to make a judgment either for or against the god? Most modern criticism has supposed that he did: either that he approved of Dionysus, and that this entailed some kind of reversal of his earlier ambivalence toward the Olympian deities; or that he disapproved of him, and was now extending that ambivalence to a wider field. Implied approval has been rejected on the ground that at the end of the play some sympathy seems to be shown for Cadmus and the other survivors, even Agaue, whereas the god is accused by Cadmus of being too human in his anger, to which he can only reply that "long ago Zeus my father approved these things" (1349). Yet naturally the dramatist dwells on the unhappiness into which his human characters are cast; that is what makes the action tragic and pathetic, and any Greek playwright, whatever his feelings about the behaviour of the god, would have done the same. Even less persuasive is the complementary contention that Pentheus is in some way a sympathetic figure and therefore his divine antagonist unsympathetic. Admittedly, as ruler of Thebes, Pentheus is not necessarily wrong by human standards in trying to control anarchy; but from the beginning he shows himself as harsh, dictatorial, and utterly incapable of understanding the forces working on his subjects. Almost every sentence he utters shows him to be unattractive and equivocal, and meant by the poet to be so.

In short, there is no evidence whatever that Euripides intended any strong criticism of Dionysus or any defence of Pentheus. But was he, on the other hand, trying to defend the practice of ecstatic religion? This seems equally unlikely, in spite of the favourable atmosphere created by the Chorus in the earlier odes. Certainly our sympathies are on the side of Dionysus, especially in the beginning; but he is so remote, so relaxed, so divinely or infernally clever that it is hard to see him as a serious object of worship. He is, it is true, a god, and there are clear signs that Euripides meant to emphasize his divine inscrutability as well as his absolute power. At the same time he seems too devious to earn anything like religious awe, and the progress of the choral songs—their rising note of harshness, admittedly in response to worsening circumstances—can hardly be intended to confirm a feeling of unusual respect.

Or is the god, as Dodds believes, "beyond good and evil"? In a way this is surely so; in a way his vengeance, needlessly cruel as it may be, accords with those natural laws of which the Chorus sings and which were sanctioned by all the Greek gods and accepted without question by most of their human worshippers: "The gods keep hidden in subtle ways the long foot of time, and hunt down the impious one; for never must a man conceive and practice what is 'better' than the laws . . ." (888–92). Euripides is not concerned here with exercising irony, as he was in his *Ion* at the expense of a semipolitical Apollo. Dionysus in the emotions he instils far more closely resembles the goddesses of *Hippolytus*, Aphrodite and Artemis, the sources of passion and chastity. Neither he nor they are held up to any kind of reprobation at the end of these plays; in *Hippolytus* there is a trace of irony at Artemis' withdrawal from the suffering and death of Hippolytus, her favourite, but the irony is wistful, resigned, almost affectionate. That is how gods are. There is a hint of a similar feeling in *The Bacchae*, although affection is absent; here the divine epiphany is starker and in a way more perfunctory (although a textual lacuna leaves some uncertainty), since the god had begun to withdraw from events after the climax of Pentheus' death.

All the same, Euripides can hardly have remained morally neutral about the kind of religion Dionysus represented. The hysteria of group worship, even if it did not cultivate the extreme techniques, exaggerated or not, of mountain dancing, was not something almost inevitable, like love or jealousy; in an organized form it was quite uncommon even in wartime Athens. The Dionysus of the maenads was a god who had to be sought out and chosen, not a universal law

9

of Nature to be accepted with resignation. In his orgiastic aspect
Dionysus must surely have elicited a strong response of some kind
from so sensitive and thoughtful a person as Euripides. Two factors
are perhaps relevant. First, in Tiresias' defence at 266ff. no attempt
is made to connect Dionysiac inspiration with that of the poet, even
though many of its effects are under consideration. Admittedly it is
Tiresias, not Euripides, speaking; but if the playwright had felt that
divine possession was to be defended as a social phenomenon, if it
were an idea to which he was temperamentally sympathetic, then he
would surely have introduced poetic inspiration—probably a quite
new conception at the time he wrote, and none the less attractive for
that—into Tiresias' brief. The second factor is the attitude of the
Chorus. Is their decline from professions of peace and moderation
toward the demand for bloodthirsty vengeance meant to be simply
a reflex of their worsening situation and the imminence of danger;
or is it a comment on the nature of Dionysiac worship itself, on its
ambiguity and internal inconsistency? Or are their moralizings to
be seen rather as part of the archaic and Aeschylean colouring of the
play as a whole? Not merely that, I think, for they are too protracted
and too emphatic to be incidental. The exact weighting of each of
these considerations is a matter for personal taste, but I feel sure that
each of them, including the second, is relevant in some degree. If so,
then Euripides was conscious of the ambivalence of Dionysus, of the
contrast between the god of pleasant ecstasy on the one hand and
the god of the destructive powers of the earth on the other, and of
the moral and social instability of those who excessively devoted
themselves to him.

Further than this one can hardly go. There is an obvious danger
in scrutinizing the play too closely for a judgment and a moral. A great
part of the force of *The Bacchae*, as of most other surviving tragedies,
lies in its dramatic unfolding of events that needed no commentary.
Euripides is retelling a familiar and complex myth. He almost certainly developed new emphases, invented a few fresh details, perhaps
gave a new emotional impetus to the story—but did he have to
possess a very distinctive and clear-cut moral attitude toward its subject? Admittedly it is hard to imagine Euripides, of all people, not
having a personal viewpoint. But he was a dramatist as well as an
intellectual; not all his plays take sides; and often his main moral

purpose is no more and no less than to present some uncomfortable truth about the world, about human nature, and about the necessities with which man is entangled. Many of the archetypal tensions of life are implicit, and not by accident, in the myths that form the material of tragedy. Critics of tragedy tend to take one or the other of two contrary attitudes toward the myths: either that they were followed by the dramatists almost slavishly and that problems of interpretation can be solved by referring to details better known to an ancient audience than to us, or on the other hand that the myth was a mere point of departure and that each surviving play contains in itself the answers to its own apparent problems. Both attitudes are too simple, at least for most of the tragedies that have survived; but the second has the attraction of allowing great subtleties of interpretation, whereas the first seems by modern critical standards coarse and too pragmatic. Nevertheless many difficulties are at least as well explained on this former premise as on the assumption of some complex and obscure personal intention by the playwright; and this seems to be the case even with such a well-known supposed problem-play as Alcestis, the earliest of Euripides' surviving dramas. In the case of The Bacchae I believe that many, though not all, of our apparent uncertainties would be removed if we had, for instance, all or most of Aeschylus' Dionysus plays. The poet's own attitude to the god might still, I suspect, remain a little elusive—because the play may not have been intended to reveal any sharply defined approach to Dionysus beyond that of a highly intellectual and somewhat quizzical observer, one who was conscious of the inconsistency of human beliefs, of the vagaries of the human psyche in contact with its own irrationality and its intractable environment.

It is easy to be too positivistic, but I retain a degree of reserve about such attractive modern judgments as the following: "What the [parodos] of the Bacchae depicts is hysteria subdued to the service of religion; what happened on Mount Cithaeron was hysteria in the raw, the dangerous Bacchism which descends as a punishment on the too respectable and sweeps them away against their will." [2] Or again: "If I understand early Dionysiac ritual aright, its social function was essentially cathartic, in the psychological sense: it purged the

---

[2] Dodds, *The Greeks and the Irrational*, pp. 272f.

individual of those infectious irrational impulses which, when dammed up, had given rise, as they have done in other cultures, to outbreaks of dancing mania and similar manifestations of collective hysteria; it relieved them by providing them with a ritual outlet." [3] On the first statement I would comment that the usual punishment of those who resist emotion, literature notwithstanding, is not hysteria in the raw, a violent but temporary attack of the emotion that is being suppressed, but rather a kind of psychosis whose operation takes on a quite different outward form from that of the suppressed emotion. Moreover I doubt whether we can see the development of these rites in terms of a social function quite as simply as the second passage suggests. In fact we know almost nothing about early Dionysiac ritual, and Dodds is only able to quote verse 77 of *The Bacchae*, "with reverent purifications," in support of his intuition, apart from two even weaker pieces of late evidence. That the service of Dionysus must have brought a sense of release from the narrowness of the ordinary life of a Greek housewife, it would be absurd to deny; but the rest does not necessarily follow. How the communal rituals began and how many people they affected remain a mystery, and my guess is that the origins and nature of Dionysiac worship were both more complex and less consonant with Freudian interpretations of Euripides' play than Dodds implies. Admittedly the excesses of Cithaeron include elements that must have been derived from a keen observation of orgiastic rites; yet it is doubtful whether we can necessarily go so far as to consider them "hysteria in the raw," that is, representative of a universal potentiality of human nature, of which "white" maenadism, as of the parodos, is the cultured relic. Is it not equally possible that Euripides arrived at his description of the scenes on Cithaeron by deliberately exaggerating some of the known tendencies of an orgiastic cult, at the same time as he developed the common theme whereby an offender against a god is punished by mistaking the identity of, and so killing, someone he loves? The human victim is as likely to be an invention of Euripides or some earlier elaborator of the basic myth as it is to be a relic, as Dodds thinks probable, of a stage when human sacrifice was actually practised in the name of Dionysus.

---

[3] *Ibid.*, p. 76.

The emotions of his worshippers lead us back to the character of the god himself as Euripides depicted him. It is in the relation of Dionysus to Pentheus that his character manifests itself in *The Bacchae*; the relation is that of the hunter to his quarry, and this is the image that underlies the whole action. The development of the image reflects the complex nature of a relationship central to the play as a whole.

At the beginning the hunter is not Dionysus but Pentheus, and the disguised god is cast as the victim: so at 434f. the servant tells the king, "See, Pentheus, we have hunted down this prey against whom you sent us." There is something strange about this pursuit, however —"This beast, we found, was gentle" (435); but Pentheus thinks he is firmly caught: "he is in my net and cannot escape me, however swift he is" (451f.). The transition from hunted to hunter is indirectly suggested for the first time at 731f. when Agaue calls on her maenads: "O my coursing hounds, we are hunted by these men"; the hounds are themselves being hunted, but they turn on the shepherds and put them to flight. Now Dionysus is explicitly established as hunter, and at 848 he announces that Pentheus "is moving into the net." This spurs the Chorus to sing of freedom, to wonder whether they will dance "like a fawn playing in the green pleasures of a meadow when it has escaped the terrifying hunt, beyond the watchers, over the well-woven nets; and, shouting, the huntsman tautens the hounds to their fastest speed" (866–72). In retrospect the hunter is still Pentheus; but the roles have already been reversed in accordance with the rule stated by the Chorus at 888–90: "The gods keep hidden in subtle ways the long foot of time, and hunt down the impious one." Soon they are calling openly on Dionysus: "around the hunter of bacchants with smiling face cast your noose; under the deadly herd of maenads let him fall!" (1020–23). Here the former hunter, Pentheus, is to be hunted, and the quarry has taken his place as hunter; and this ambivalence of status is repeated more obscurely with the maenads themselves, for as they fell upon the cattle on Cithaeron so they are to fall on their would-be hunter, Pentheus, as a "deadly herd." The cattle, normally docile victims of aggression, are stampeded into frenzy and become accessories of the hunter. Now begins a new series of uses of the metaphor in which Pentheus is definitely and decisively the prey. He is the "mounted beast" of 1108, his head on Agaue's thyrsus is like that of a lion in 1142, and Agaue calls on the god as "fellow-hunter, fellow-worker in the kill" at 1146; "a fortunate quarry indeed!" she says at 1184, and "The Bacchic huntsman wisely, cleverly swung his maenads upon this beast" (1189–91), to which the Chorus replies, "For our lord is a hunter" (1192); so too in Agaue's boast that she has hunted down the quarry with bare hands and torn it apart (1203–10, 1237). A final irony, and a subtle reference to Pentheus' initial role, is seen in Agaue's wish of 1252–56: "Would that my child were a successful hunter, made like his mother in his ways, whenever in company with the young Thebans he went after beasts! But fighting against gods is all *he* can do."

The image reproduces, on a different level, the changes in the relations between Dionysus and Pentheus. It is used to emphasize some of these changes, and especially the aspect of reversal; and it deepens our apprehension of the god's inexorable revenge as the play develops. It also helps to establish the position of the two groups of bacchants: first the true ones, the Chorus of Lydian women, who resemble the fawn that has escaped the hunter; then the abnormally frenzied women of Cithaeron who rehearse, by their preliminary attack on the villages and the cattle, the eventual hunting down of Pentheus. In all this the image acts as a kind of counterpoint, even if it discloses no radically new information about the two characters. Dionysus has allowed himself to be hunted down and insulted; he uses his divine powers to escape and gradually makes his captor into a ready victim for his instruments, the "deadly herd," Agaue's "coursing hounds." Pentheus' temporal authority is progressively revealed as impotence in relation to the unfolding power of the god; and since king and god are in direct conflict it follows that the victim will become the aggressor, the hunted the hunter, and vice versa.

Even apart from the reciprocity implied in this reversal of roles there are some curious points of contact between Pentheus and Dionysus. We should expect them to be utterly different types, but in fact they have much in common. They are, of course, first cousins and roughly of the same age. Dionysus has long hair and is attractive to women; Pentheus is interested in sex and takes great delight in his female clothes. He is dressed as a bacchant, as a worshipper of the god, before he is killed, and his climbing of the fir tree and pelting with

14

branches might reflect Dionysiac ritual (although see notes on 1070, 1096ff.); in certain Hellenistic cults masks of the god were hung in trees. His genealogical descent from Echion is emphasized, and thus his monstrous, chthonic, and snake-like character. This connects him with Dionysus, who is also, through Semele, descended from the Sown Men, and is seen as a snake by his snake-handling worshippers. Agaue believes Pentheus' head to be that of a young lion, another of Diony-sus' animal manifestations, rather as Pentheus himself had seen Dionysus as a bull.

Let us take note of these correspondences, but not exaggerate their significance. They do not of themselves imply that Pentheus was an aspect or perverted double of the god—though it may be relevant that according to Strabo the Phrygians compared Lycurgus, the Thracian victim of Dionysus and counterpart of Pentheus, with the god himself, and Nonnus ascribes to Lycurgus an actual cult. That Pentheus was Dionysus' cousin and his rough contemporary arises from the family relationships established for independent reasons in the cycle of Theban myths. His obsession with the bacchants' sup-posed immorality and drunkenness may be based on popular criticism of orgiastic rites and the abuse of wine and need not label him as especially Dionysiac by nature. His dressing as a bacchant is an apt refinement of a common theme, the killing by mistake of an unrecog-nized relative or lover. It may, it is true, also reflect the practice of dressing a sacrificial victim as a devotee or associate, whether human or animal, of a god, and this kind of motive could account, too, for conceivably ritual tree-climbing and hurling of missiles. Pentheus' chthonic, monstrous, and snake-like aspects ally him with his divine cousin, but then all the members of the house of Cadmus inevitably had these associations, which are understandably stressed by the Chorus. And Agaue's seeing him as a lion is natural enough, for what is torn to pieces in the ritual *sparagmos* is an animal that espe-cially represents the potency of the god.

There is great subtlety and complexity, as well as great irony, in Euripides' description of the two opponents and their relationship; but although Pentheus may be thought of as dedicated to Dionysus as his victim by being dressed in the ritual apparel of Dionysus' wor-shippers, there is little real evidence that he is a kind of aberrant incar-nation of the power and personality of the god himself. Indeed it is probable from Dionysus' prophecies at the play's end, fragmentary though they are, and from Cadmus' reactions to them, that Pentheus is not to be awarded a cult or regarded as anything but criminally deluded; this distinguishes him from Lycurgus, even supposing the late evidence for Lycurgus' cult to be correct. Thus, like the reversal of roles in the image of the hunter and his quarry, the other ties and tensions between the two opponents, together with those between foreigner and Hellene, mortal and immortal, disguised and undisguised, seem primarily intended to make the most of the dramatic situation presupposed in the traditional myth.

These tensions were in their own right an integral part of the tragedy. It can be seen from Euripides' other surviving plays that the *agon*, the contest or conflict between two characters representing opposite points of view, was for him, even more than for Sophocles or Aeschylus, a central part of the drama. The impact of the sophists and a growing public interest in the techniques of argument gave the Euripidean *agon* an especially forensic quality. In *The Bacchae* the shades of the great sophists Protagoras and Gorgias lurk behind scenes whose character may puzzle or disappoint the modern reader. The time and energy devoted by Euripides to the exposition of apparently trivial arguments (like some of those deployed by Tiresias) can only be understood either as a parody of the sophistic style or as a passing exercise in the genre. Both Euripides and his audiences were obviously fascinated by the new approaches to the problem of "making the worse case the better": approaches that depended on typical sophistic attitudes to the meaning of words, to the ambiguities of syntax, and to the foundations of morality which they saw as solely conventional. This kind of fascination is one important reason for the arguments and counterarguments, often in a series of single-verse utterances, that punctuate the action—in the efforts of Cadmus and Tiresias to persuade Pentheus, in the clash of wills between Cadmus and the mad Agaue, and above all in the central conflict between Pentheus and Dionysus. The opportunity for a prolonged and developing confrontation between the disturbing new cult of a highly irregular deity and the compounded force of reaction, perversity, and authority must have been greatly to Euripides' taste.

The conflict ends with Pentheus' death and dismemberment some two-thirds of the way through the play, and this is followed by

Agaue's self-recognition and despair. The first of these great climaxes, in accordance with the limitations and conventions of the ancient theatre, takes place offstage and is reported at length by a Messenger. His speech, with its predecessor and complement in which the first attack by the maenads is described, constitutes the pivotal point of the drama. It is a sign both of the intrinsic compulsion of the Pentheus story and of Euripides' narrative genius that two long set speeches, each by a more or less anonymous character, can carry on so successfully the momentum of the action with no decline in tension and no strong effect of artificiality. A sense of unreality there may be; but this was needed to convey the fantastic quality of the events on the mountain.

The messenger-speeches that report the action on Cithaeron are separated by another important climax that takes place in Thebes itself and is directly represented on the stage: the completion of Dionysus' infatuation of Pentheus and the preparation of the victim for his journey to his death. This in turn is more narrowly enclosed by two choral odes, the Third and Fourth Stasima, which invoke divine punishment for excess and then call more clearly for bloody vengeance. Outside the messenger-speeches, again, lie two secondary climaxes: first the palace miracles—the blazing up of fire, the earthquake and the divine voice, the terror of the Chorus; and second the entrance of Agaue carrying her son's head, her gradual return to sanity, and her horror at what madness has produced. Each is a scene of extraordinary theatrical power and deep emotion. Thus after the Prologue and the long opening scenes and choral songs, which establish the nature of the bacchants' worship and the conflict between Pentheus and the god, the play advances in a series of carefully related climaxes to the final scenes of prophecy and despair. The climaxes arise naturally and inevitably, and their emotional and dramaturgical quality is varied with great artistry. Here Euripides may take full credit. The palace miracles had been used by Aeschylus, and the murder of Pentheus belonged to the most basic form of the myth; but the preliminary attack on the cattle, the raid on the villages, the dressing up of Pentheus, and the elaboration of Agaue's return to her senses, although they may have been represented in the tradition, clearly owe much of their power to the poet himself.

The dramatic forcefulness of *The Bacchae* depends to an im-

portant extent on its constant reiteration of conflict within a sym-
metrical structure of direct and indirect climaxes. Beyond these, the
movement is maintained by the careful placing and unusual relevance
of the choral odes, in what amounts to a return to the most classical
form of tragedy. The archaizing tone that this and other structural
and metrical qualities impart to the play gives rise to a tension between form and content which is both curiously satisfying and at the
same time rather mysterious. A different kind of duality appears in
the whole conflict between Dionysus and Pentheus, between irresisti-
ble god and recalcitrant mortal. Yet a third kind, the most subtle and
profound of all, lies in the nature of Dionysus himself. He brings both
joy and grief, calmness and dangerous excitement, life and death.
Both smiling and cruel, he is neither Olympian nor entirely
chthonian; his fertility infuses the vine, but also the bull, and is
celebrated in the tearing up and devouring of animals. He inspires the
Chorus to some of the most moving devotional poetry that has survived from the ancient world, and some of the most inconsistent
and self-deluding claptrap in all the history of religions. It is these
dualities, together with its intrinsic dramatic quality and its perfec-
tion of form and expression, that make *The Bacchae* one of the
greatest tragedies ever written.

NOTE ON THE TRANSLATION

The translation follows the Greek text extremely closely, and
each verse in Greek is represented by a corresponding line—which is
not meant to be poetical—in English. Occasionally, part of the content
of two verses is transposed in order to achieve an acceptable English
word order; but the sense of the Greek words and the shape of each
Greek sentence have only been sacrificed where absolutely necessary
in favour of over-all nuance of meaning. At the same time I have tried,
sometimes in vain, to make this very literal translation sound reasonably fluent in English. In the choral odes this has not been too difficult, since they are so intrinsically poetical that they fall into a kind
of free poetry even in close translation. Parts of the dialogue, on the
other hand, will seem strange and stilted. Often this reproduces a similar quality in the Greek, since tragic dialogue is sometimes like that
—deliberately so at times, but at other times not. Yet even in other

passages the English has often acquired a kind of woodenness that is not there in the Greek, and here the ambition to be literal is the main culprit. Other translations are available in which fluidity of thought and expression may be more consistently achieved, though at considerable cost in accuracy and tone. Of the two evils between which the translator has to choose, I decided that lack of naturalness in some of the dialogue was, for present purposes, the lesser.

NOTE ON THE GREEK TEXT USED

For the sake of accuracy and for the benefit of a small minority of specialist readers I list below a number of readings accepted for my translation where the text might be in doubt. Only rarely do these represent departures from the text favoured by E. R. Dodds *in his commentary*. (It should be observed that the text printed in his edition is that of Gilbert Murray's *Oxford Classical Text*, on which he generally improves.) Occasionally I have noted places where I retain Murray's text. In other disputed places it will be obvious which text I translate.

95	*thalamois*	against Wecklein, Murray.
115	*eut' an*	(Elmsley).
135	*hos an*	(Gompf), doubtfully.
200	*ouden sophizomestha*	with mss. and Murray.
335	*Semeles*	with mss. and Dodds, against Murray and most editors.
427	*sopha d'*	with Dindorf, Dodds, with a stop after 426.
461	*ouk oknos*	with Wakefield, Meurig-Davies, Dodds.
466	*autos m'*	with P. Ant. for mss. *hēmas.*
506	*outh' . . . outh'*	with P. Ant.
571–73		I accept Wilamowitz' rearrangement, with Murray, against Dodds.
738	*echousan*	with mss. and Murray, against Reiske, Dodds.
816	*d'*	with ms., against Musurus, Murray.
860	*hōs pephuken entelēs*	with Dobree and Hirzel against ms. *hos . . . en telei.*

19

1002-7		I accept Murray's text except for Dodds' *sōphronism'* for ms. *sōphrona* in 1002 and *phanera th', hōs agein* for ms. *phanera tōn aei* in 1007.
1026	*opheos*	with ms. and Dodds against Wilamowitz, Murray (*Opheos*).
1090f.	*hēssona*	(Heath), *echousai* (ms.) against Murray, Dodds.
1103	*druinois ... kladois*	after Hartung.
1147	*hēi*	with ms., against Reiske, Murray, Dodds.
1152	*chrēma*	with Dodds, against Orion, Murray.
1157	*Haida*	with Wilamowitz, Dodds.
1162	*goon*	with Canter, Dodds, against Murray.
1164	*teknōi*	with Kirchhoff, against ms., Murray, Dodds.
1174	*leontos agroterou*	after Murray, *exempli gratia*.
1229	*drumois*	with ms., Dodds, against Bruhn, Murray.
1312	*elambanen*	with ms., Dodds, against Hermann, Murray.

CHARACTERS

AGAUE, daughter of CADMUS and mother of PENTHEUS

CADMUS, former king of Thebes and father of AGAUE

CHORUS, female bacchants from Lydia

DIONYSUS, disguised for most of the play as a Lydian Stranger, leader of the CHORUS of bacchants

MESSENGER

PENTHEUS, king of Thebes and son of AGAUE

SECOND MESSENGER

SERVANT

TIRESIAS, a famous Theban seer

THE BACCHAE

The scene: before the royal palace at Thebes. A
tomb and a ruined house are represented on
one side of the stage. The god DIONYSUS enters,
disguised as the male leader of a group of foreign women from Lydia who are bacchants, followers of the god.

DIONYSUS   *I have come, the son of Zeus, to this land of the*
   Thebans,
I, Dionysus, whom once Cadmus' daughter bore,

---

1   Most Greek plays begin with a dialogue, or a direct address to the audience. Its purpose is to describe briefly the
background, both physical and narrative, of the action.
Euripides favoured the direct address, as here. The effect is artificial—less so with a god, perhaps, than with a human character; but the device spares the audience both confusion and unnecessary delay in starting the action. In any case Greek tragedy
did not aim at great, or at least consistent, realism.

There is a conspicuous resemblance between this prologue
by the god DIONYSUS and that by Aphrodite in *Hippolytus*, written by Euripides some twenty years earlier. The
two plays have similar themes—punishment for the rejection of
a deity who represents an emotion, whether it be the passion of
love as in *Hippolytus* or religious ecstasy as in *The Bacchae*. In

Semele, brought to childbed by lightning-carried fire.

---

each case the prologue predicts the general outcome of events, though with one or two concealments or false clues. The general outline of the plot must have been known to the audience in advance, but individual refinements and innovations were always possible, especially with Euripides. The story of DIONYSUS, his birth, cult, and overcoming of the resistance to his worship in Hellas, must have been unusually familiar: Aeschylus, in particular, had composed no less than two tetralogies (groups of four plays) on these themes (see also pages 2–3).

An important distinction separates DIONYSUS here from gods in other prologues: he will act as a direct *human* agent in the punishment of PENTHEUS and Thebes; he will not just influence events from on high. Instead he is disguised as the foreign and exotic male leader of a company of female devotees of DIONYSUS, "bacchae" or bacchants, who have followed him from Asia Minor (where the cult is thought to have started) and who are now uneasy visitors in Thebes (see notes on 5, 23). They form the CHORUS of the play and give it its name; they take an important part in it, not in the sense of rushing around doing things, but rather by describing Dionysiac worship from within (their most serious function), by providing normative responses to events, and by calling for action against PENTHEUS when it becomes necessary. In this, as in many other formal aspects of the play, Euripides reverts to the fashion of earlier days. By the time he wrote *The Bacchae*, near the end of his life in 407 B.C. (it was not actually produced in Athens until 405), the chorus had generally become otiose, primarily a source of short, digressionary odes to separate scenes of action.

The metre of the prologue is the regular metre of dialogue in tragedy, the iambic trimeter, based on three double-iambic measures. The iamb is basically composed of a short syllable followed by a long one, and Greek verse was *quantitative*—that is, its rhythm depended on the relation of long and short syllables (in terms of duration), not on an independent stress-accent as in English verse.

3ff Semele is described as a mortal princess, but there are signs in

24

Exchanging my divine form for a mortal one
I am here, by the streams of Dirce and the waters of Ismenus;   5
and I see the tomb of my mother, the thunderbolt-struck,
here by the palace, and the ruins of her house
smouldering with the still-living flame of the fire of Zeus—
Hera's undying outrage against my mother.

---

literature and cult that she was regarded as a Persephone-like figure who came to life again and was worshipped together with DIONYSUS (e.g., Pindar, *Olympians* 2, 25ff., Theocritus, *Idylls* 26, 5f., and 998 of *The Bacchae* itself). Learned writers in antiquity treated her as an earth-goddess, which may be right; she is thought to have been Asiatic in origin and may well have been associated with DIONYSUS in the Lydian or Phrygian fertility-cult that gave rise to Dionysiac religion in its Greek form. It has been suggested that her blasting by lightning originally signified the fertilization of earth by the sky/lightning/rain-god, but this must remain doubtful.

4   To avoid confusion DIONYSUS stresses both here and at 53f. that he has taken on completely human form and is disguised as the mortal leader of a band of Asiatic bacchants. At the end of the play he will appear again without disguise; but even during the action his role is often ambiguous. This not only provides a piquant irony and reinforces the dualities in which the play abounds (p. 18), but it also helps to produce a mysterious uncertainty about where the natural ends and the supernatural begins.

5   Dirce and Ismenus were the two rivers of Thebes. The town was built on a low hill in the fertile plain of Boeotia, and lay some ten miles from Mount Cithaeron—often mentioned in the play—which dominates it to the south. It had been important in the late Bronze Age, the era in which the Theban cycle of myths, and indeed almost all other Greek myths, are set. But it was remembered that Thebes was destroyed by civil dispute some time before the Trojan War and long before the fall of Mycenae, which seems to be historically correct.

6ff   The scenery in Greek drama was slight, so some description is

I commend Cadmus, who has made this ground sacrosanct,   10
his daughter's precinct; and with the vine's
clustering verdure I have covered it round.
   I left behind the gold-bearing acres of the Lydians
and Phrygians, passed through the sun-beaten plains of the
    Persians,
and Bactrian walled cities, and that wintry land   15
of the Medes, and prosperous Arabia,

---

necessary. On the stage can be seen a precinct containing Semele's tomb and the ruins of her house, struck by lightning from Zeus and still, miraculously, smoking—although the smoke is probably to be imagined for most of the play. CADMUS had walled the place off, because of family piety and because things struck by lightning were regarded as sacrosanct. DIONYSUS has made a vine grow there—one of his sacred plants, for its greenness and fertility as well as for its grapes and wine. At the back of the stage, as we learn at 591 and 1214, is the façade of the royal palace, home of PENTHEUS.

10 CADMUS is the legendary founder of Thebes and father of Semele, AGAUE, Ino, Autonoe, and the boy Actaeon (the first and last of these now dead), and the grandfather of PENTHEUS, AGAUE's son, to whom, in the absence of a living son of his own, he has handed over the royal power in his old age.

13– Athenian audiences seem to have been especially interested in
19 details of foreign lands. Colonial expansion—first to the eastern Aegean seaboard from around 1000 B.C., then to the Black Sea and the Levant, and westward to Sicily and southern Italy, from around 750 B.C.—gave the subject a perennial and almost a family interest. In the fifth century there were two fresh motives for curiosity: first, the repulse of the Persian invasions between 491 and 479 B.C. produced a new kind of interest about the defeated "barbarian"; and second, the sophistic movement evinced a strong preoccupation with comparative ethnology and the collection of details about foreign lands and customs, partly with the intention of showing that "law" is a relative

and all Asia which along the salt sea
lies, with mingled Hellenes and barbarians together
its fair-towered cities filled,
and to this land of the Hellenes I first came   20
when there, in Asia, I had set my dances, established my

---

concept. The histories of Herodotus are another example of
this kind of ethnological and geographical interest.

There is, in addition, a particular point to the geographical
excursus here. The cult of DIONYSUS was known to have come
to Greece from abroad, either by way of Thrace or directly, as
Euripides assumes, from Lydia and Phrygia (roughly east-cen-
tral and central Asia Minor respectively). The *gold-bearing
acres* of 13 refer to the auriferous sands of the Lydian river
Pactolus; the hot plains of Persia, the forts of Bactria, the hard
winters of Media, the prosperous incense-coast of Arabia likewise reveal a little real knowledge. Euripides mentions them
partly for their exotic connotations and partly to emphasize how far over Asia the rites of DIONYSUS were held to have
spread.

17– The cities on the eastern Aegean coast were Greek colonies that
19 also contained, or were surrounded by, a more or less sub-
servient barbarian population. "Barbarian" for a Greek signified
the speaking of a foreign tongue, which sounded ungainly and
stammering—hence, probably, the reduplicative term *barbaros*.
The chronology here is poetical, since these colonies were not
founded earlier than about 1000 B.C., whereas the setting of the
play precedes the Trojan War and belongs some three centuries
earlier. Most Greeks, even after the work of Herodotus and
Thucydides, were vague about their past and had no specific
chronological guides apart from speculative lists of Olympic
victors or Spartan kings.

21 *I had set my dances:* dancing was part of the worship of DIO-
NYSUS, as was going to the mountains and occasionally rending
and eating the flesh of animals. All these things released a special strength, abolished inhibitions, and united the worshippers
with each other and with the power and freedom of Nature.

27

rituals, to be a manifest god to men.
Thebes here was the first in this Hellenic land
that I made shriek in ecstasy, that I clothed with the fawnskin,
and gave the thyrsus into their hand, the ivy spear;   25
since my mother's sisters, who least should have done so,
denied that Dionysus was son of Zeus—
said that Semele was brided by some mortal man
and then attributed to Zeus the error of her bed,
by a clever idea of Cadmus. For this reason, they were always
        proclaiming,   30
Zeus slew her, because she falsely said he was her lover.

---

22   *a manifest god to men:* DIONYSUS was one of the more recent
     additions to the Greek pantheon. He is mentioned only glanc-
     ingly in Homer; but his name occurs on a Linear B tablet from
     Crete, and his worship might have entered Greece as early as
     the end of the Bronze Age. Interest in it was evidently renewed
     with the wave of irrationalism associated with the stagnation of
     Athens as the Peloponnesian War dragged to its catastrophic
     end in 405 B.C.

23   Thebes was one of the most powerful cities of Achaean or My-
     cenaean (i.e., late Bronze Age) Greece, until its destruction (see
     note on 5). Its visible remains today are slight, since the ugly
     modern town is built over the ancient site. It had some special
     connection with DIONYSUS, as is shown by the story of his birth
     there. Perhaps the Asiatic cult really did take root in Thebes
     before other places in Greece.

24f The "shriek of ecstasy," *ololugē* in Greek, is a special woman's
     cry of triumph. The fawnskin was ritual Dionysiac wear, em-
     phasizing the connection of the worshipper with the world of
     Nature. The *thyrsus*, for which there is no English word, is a
     staff (properly a fennel rod or cane, and often so termed later
     in the play) with ivy tied to its top. It was the particular identi-
     fying mark of the devotee of DIONYSUS and was waved up and
     down or struck on the ground as the ecstatic dance proceeded.

26ff *my mother's sisters:* Ino and Autonoe (see note on 10). We
     shall learn at 35 that the god has driven all the women of

28

So them I stung in madness from their homes
and they dwell on the mountain stricken in their wits;
I compelled them to wear the apparel proper to my rites,
and all the female seed of the Cadmeians, all   35
of the women, I maddened from their homes;
together with the children of Cadmus, mingled with them,
under the green firs they sit on rocks, with no roof above.
For this land must learn to the full, even against its will,
that it is uninitiated in my bacchic rites;   40
and I must speak in defence of my mother Semele
by appearing to mortals as the god she bore to Zeus.
    Now Cadmus has given his prerogatives as king
to Pentheus, his daughter's son,
who fights the gods by refusing my worship, and thrusts me   45
away from his libations, and nowhere addresses me in his
    prayers.

Thebes, not only the princesses, out of their wits. Formally the
princesses are maddened for propagating the malicious rumour
about Semele's pregnancy, the others as part of the punishment
of PENTHEUS (45–48). These Theban women are no ordinary
bacchants; they are "maddened" (32f., 36) far beyond the normal degree of Dionysiac inspiration—which did not lead to the
tearing apart of cattle or the ravaging of villages (735ff., 751ff.).
The CHORUS, on the contrary, are true bacchants, and the worship they long for, though it includes the eating of raw flesh,
has little of the murderous, sinister, and anti-social excesses of
the women of Thebes.

35f all of the women: literally, "as many as were women," a typical
     Euripidean redundancy, emphasizing at least that it was the
     women and not the men who were infatuated.

38   rocks, with no roof above: literally, "on [and not 'among,' as
     nearly all editors have assumed] roofless rocks." "Roofless" is
     most probably a transferred epithet that applies to the bac-
     chants as a whole: they are sitting around in the open air, and
     on rocks at that—not, as Theban women normally would be,
     at home.

29

For this reason I shall show myself to be a god, to him
and to all the Thebans. To another land,
when I have put things here to rights, I shall direct my feet,
revealing my true self; but if the citizens of Thebes   50
seek in anger and by arms to bring the bacchants from the
      mountain,
I shall join battle with them at the head of my maenads.
For this reason I have changed to mortal appearance
and altered my shape to human form.
    But you who have left Tmolus, mountain barrier of Lydia,   55
my band of worshippers, you women whom from among the
      foreigners
I brought with me, companions in rest and in travel,

50f This never happens in the play, though it is envisaged at 780ff.
It is perhaps mentioned to titillate the audience with the pos-
sibility of an unusual development; but such a version is depicted on pots of the fourth century B.C., and probably a variant
of this kind was known even in Euripides' time.

55 *Tmolus:* the mountain range to the south of Sardis, capital of
Lydia; see 462f.

56 *band of worshippers:* the word *thiasos,* which may have been
Asiatic in origin, occurs frequently in the play, and is almost a
technical term for a group of bacchants (who were mainly, but
not necessarily, women) united in the worship of DIONYSUS.
Judging from inscriptions later than Euripides, when the worship of DIONYSUS became highly organized, each city tended to
have three *thiasoi,* each with a male leader or *exarchos.* The
idea of the *exarchos* is important in the ode that follows;
DIONYSUS, in his human guise, is the leader of the *thiasos* from
Lydia, and as the ecstasy grows the god himself is envisaged as
spurring on his worshippers. His address to the CHORUS here is a
formal way of preparing their entrance; they are not meant to
hear 59, for example, which would reveal to them the secret
that their leader is the god himself.

57 *companions . . . travel:* based on J. E. Sandys, this translation
conveys something of the almost pedantically and prosaically

lift up the drums that are native in the land
of the Phrygians, the invention of mother Rhea and myself,
and, surrounding these royal halls   60
of Pentheus, strike them, that the city of Cadmus may see!
And I shall go to the folds of Cithaeron,
where the bacchants are, and share in their dances.

CHORUS   *From Asian land*

---

explicit quality of the Greek phrase, which uses a pair of long,
compound, verbal adjectives, literally "sitting-beside and jour-
neying-together-with." The analysis of the concept "constant
companions" into its binary components serves to stress the
devotion of this particular group and that it had come from
overseas; it also illustrates the fifth-century interest in classifica-
tion on the one hand and rhetorical antithetical analysis on the
other.

58f The *drums* are like tambourines and were used in several different orgiastic cults. Together with the skirl of the flute they
expressed the excitement of the worshippers and reflected the
rhythm of their ecstatic dances (cf. 127f.). *Rhea* was sister and
wife of Kronos and mother of Zeus; according to one account
Zeus was born in Crete, and his infant cries were hidden from
his father (who was in the habit of eating his children) by the
Couretes, young demons who beat on drums for this purpose,
and later established the drum in rites for Rhea the mother.
This is described more fully in the ode that follows (120–34),
which also attempts to show, by conflating several similar cults,
how the drum came to be associated with DIONYSUS.

64ff The *Parodos*, or ode of entry, is sung by the CHORUS as it
enters the orchestra, or circular dancing floor, through one or
other of the passageways at each side. The present ode consists
of a prelude, two balanced pairs of stanzas, and a longer conclusion, or epode. Each pair of stanzas contains a "strophe" and
"antistrophe," named after the "turns" and "counterturns" ex-
ecuted by the dancers. Metrical and choreographic correspon-
dence was precisely maintained between each paired strophe
and antistrophe, though rhythm and therefore dance move-

ment usually change between each pair.

The lyric metre (which is again quantitative—see end of note on 1) is varied. The prelude and first strophic pair are primarily made up of Ionic dimeters, basically ⌣ ⌣ – – | ⌣ ⌣ – –, an excited rhythm suitable for ecstatic songs and therefore unusually common in *The Bacchae*. (No attempt to reproduce these rhythms is made in the essentially prose translation, except by indenting to correspond with changes of metre and verse length in the Greek.) The second strophic pair is in a more complicated combination of metres, primarily "Aeolic" in character (so termed because found in the lyric poems of Sappho and Alcaeus, who wrote in the Aeolic dialect of their island of Lesbos) and based on a single choriamb, – ⌣ ⌣ –, as rhythmical nucleus. The epode is especially complex. It is mainly dactylic, based on the measure – ⌣ ⌣, but has a run of Ionics (144–51) and some Aeolic verses interspersed.

I give three examples of these different types of metre with a transliteration of the Greek:

verse 83	*ĭtĕ bākchāi ĭtĕ bākchāi*	Ionic
verse 154	*Tmōlŏu chrŭsŏrhŏou chlĭdāi*	Aeolic
verse 155	*mēlpĕtĕ tŏn Dĭŏnūsŏn*	dactylic

The ode consists of (1) a call for holy silence (prelude), (2) a declaration of the blessed state of the bacchant (first strophe), (3) the story of Dionysus' birth (first antistrophe), (4) a call to Thebes to worship Dionysus (second strophe), (5) a description of how the drum became associated with the cult of Dionysus (second antistrophe), (6) further elaboration of the ecstasy of the bacchants and their male leader (epode). The ode is in fact a hymn, with ritual opening, solemn repetition of the divine name, and rehearsal of the history and cult of the god and his effect on his adorants. It also reveals a regular alternation between generalization (in the strophes) and particular detail (in the antistrophes), a simple structural device favoured in many other odes by Euripides. The effect of the whole song is tremendous: it conveys the power and beauty of

having passed sacred Tmolus I hasten   65
  in sweet toil for Bromios,
  in labour that is no labour, exalting
    the Bacchic god.
  Who is in the road, who in the road? Who   68
in the palace? Let him be present, and with a
                mouth that utters no
  impiety let each man sanctify himself.   70
  For with the ever-accustomed words
  Dionysus shall I hymn.

STROPHE 1

O
blessed he who in happiness   72

DIONYSUS' worship, the utter devotion that the god arouses, and the complex thrill of mountain dancing.

66 *Bromios:* one of DIONYSUS' cult-names, presumably meaning "the roaring one." It may be connected with the tendency to see bulls or lions as special embodiments of his power, or with the roar of thunder as Semele was struck by lightning at his birth.

67 Literally, "labour well-laboured," a figure of speech favoured by Euripides. He calls DIONYSUS "the Bacchic [god]" rather than simply "Bacchus," which occurs only once in this play. Bacchus (*Bakchos* in un-Latinized transliteration from the Greek) was probably in origin a Lydian name for the god, and it was, of course, the one by which the Romans later knew him.

68– A ritual call for attendance and the avoidance of unhallowed
70 speech as the procession advances into the orchestra.

  Who in the road: repetition was a mannerism of Euripidean lyric much parodied by Aristophanes, but this is a ritual repetition, like "to the mountain, to the mountain" at 116 and elsewhere.

  Let him be present: literally, "let him be displaced," i.e., from where he is now, implying attendance on the proceedings rather than keeping out of the way.

72– The worshipper's happiness arises from his participation in the
77 religious cult, his holy way of life (including the ritual purity

33

knowing the rituals of the gods
makes holy his way of life and

of 77), and the merging of his consciousness and personality with the other members of the band of worshippers in the mountains. This is a remarkable statement for a poet of the fifth century B.C., and it suggests a view of the psyche (the *psuche*, which I have paraphrased as "consciousness and personality" just above) not very far from that of Socrates as described in the earlier dialogues of Plato. Socrates, who was Euripides' contemporary, thought that "soul" was something to be tended and cared for, to be kept pure by honourable behaviour. To us this idea may seem commonplace, but it had a degree of novelty at a time when soul was regarded mainly as life-principle, and the archaic morality of "help your friends and damage your enemies," which was also the basis of human and divine relationships according to the ordinary Olympian religion, still persisted. Even apart from this, the recognition of the power of mass exaltation and its association with the idea of purity is of the highest interest.

Verrall's horrible translation of 75, "congregationalizes his soul," is surprisingly approved by E. R. Dodds. Indeed the use of the terminology of Victorian bishops and the like as a means of trying to reproduce the subtly but definitely non-Christian nature of Dionysiac devotion is one of the few relative failures of Dodds' exemplary edition. Thus his translation of this whole passage, "O blessed is he who, by happy favour knowing the sacraments of the gods, leads the life of holy service and is inwardly a member of God's company," seems to me quite misleading. Taking part in the devouring of raw flesh (see note on 139) among a band of ecstatic women on Mount Cithaeron was really very unlike a Christian communion or mass, even though it may have been more like it than was, say, the presentation of a new robe to Athena in her Parthenon. The very word "sacrament" is surely incorrect, unless it can be clearly shown that in eating a piece of goat the bacchants thought they were eating the god himself, or a symbol of him, rather than assimilating a bit of raw Nature.

mingles his spirit with the sacred band,   75
in the mountains serving Bacchus
with reverent purifications;
and duly observing the rites
of Cybele the Great Mother
and shaking up and down the thyrsus   80
and with ivy crowned
he worships Dionysus.
> *Onward bacchants, onward bacchants,*
> *bringing Dionysus,*
> *Bromios, god and child of a god,*   85

78– The bacchant is loosely described as also worshipping Cybele,
82 the "Great Mother" or earth-goddess of Asia. Euripides tends
to mix together, or syncretize, the ecstatic cults and makes
little distinction between the Asiatic Cybele with her Corybantes and the Cretan Rhea and her Couretes, or between the
Lydian Bacchus/Dionysus and the primarily Phrygian Cybele.
It should be noted that the bacchant is treated in this strophe
and elsewhere in the ode as male. Normally the sacred bands
seem to have been composed of women, who sometimes have a
male leader, or *exarchos*, as the CHORUS has the disguised
DIONYSUS; but male worshippers were not excluded, and it is
envisaged that "the whole land shall dance" (114), obviously
including the men. Yet the use of the masculine gender in
Greek for typical bacchants is probably a generalizing one, not
intended to exclude women—of whom, indeed, the CHORUS is
obviously thinking.

84 *bringing Dionysus*: the Greek verb can mean "bringing back"
or "bringing home," and Dodds inclines to connect it with a
festival of DIONYSUS called the *Katagōgia*, or "bringing back."
But this simply refers to the return of the god, every year or
two, to a particular shrine. In the present context the *kat-* part
of the compound verb may well have its local meaning of
"down" and may refer to bringing the god down from the
mountains of Phrygia to the (lower) streets of Greece. At the
same time DIONYSUS *is* returning to his Theban birthplace.

down from Phrygian mountains
into Hellas' broad-trodden streets,   87
Bromios the roaring one!

ANTISTROPHE 1

Whom
bearing within her, in forced   88
pangs of childbirth
when Zeus' lightning flew   90
his mother thrust premature
from the womb, and left her life
at the lightning's stroke.
Instantly into chambers of birth
Zeus son of Kronos received him,   95
and hiding him in his thigh
locks him with golden
pins, secret from Hera.
   He brought to birth, when the Fates
   accomplished the time, a bull-horned god   100
   and crowned him with garlands

96ff The Vedic god Soma, who like DIONYSUS was associated with an alcoholic drink, was inserted in the thigh of the sky-god Indra. The resemblance seems too great to be accidental, and this is one of the comparatively rare cases where talk of Indo-European diffusion of a myth is justified. According to the Greek myth the jealous Hera persuaded Semele to ask Zeus to come to her in his true form. She was consequently burned up, but Zeus snatched the embryo and brought it to completion in his own thigh.

100 *a bull-horned god*: the infatuated PENTHEUS will see DIONYSUS as a bull (618, 922), and the CHORUS will call on him to appear as a bull, a snake, or a lion (1018f.). The bull is one of the god's commonest incarnations—though it does not appear in art until after the time of this play—and expresses his power, his leadership, his potency as a force of Nature.

of snakes; for this reason the maenads
twine in their tresses
the beast-reared prey.

STROPHE 2

O Thebes who nurtured Semele,   105
be crowned with ivy;
abound, abound with evergreen
fair-berried bryony,
and devote yourselves as bacchants with twigs

102– The Greeks were interested in "explaining," often quite improb-
104   ably, the origin—whether ritual, etymological, or accidental—of
obscure or bizarre beliefs or customs; and this is a typical
"aetiological" explanation of that kind. If maenads really put
snakes (the *beast-reared prey*) in their hair it was to show
their subjection of and union with the wilder aspects of Nature;
but Euripides was himself very attracted by aetiology (see note
on 1330ff.) and could not be satisfied with this explanation. The
Greeks looked on snakes at times as ugly and dangerous (thus
they form the hair of the Gorgons and the Furies), at times as
benign, establishing a man's association with the earth or with
a particular spot (for example, in the idea of a protective
house snake) or symbolizing, by their casting off of their skin,
the birth and rebirth of the earth and its fruits. They could also
represent the more ambiguous chthonic powers of the dead
and the demons of the underworld.

105ff The second strophe continues the description of Dionysiac
worship begun in the first and urges all Thebes to join in.
Again it will be followed by a passage of aetiology in the antistrophe.

109f It is uncertain whether these *twigs* (or the Greek word can
equally mean "branches") of oak or fir are carried in the hand,
as a forerunner of or substitute for the fennel-rod thyrsus, or
whether they are woven into garlands. There is slight evidence
for each interpretation from outside the play, and within it we

> *of oak or fir,*   110
> *and cloaks of dappled fawnskin*
> *fringe all round with white tresses*
> *of wool; with violent thyrsus-rods*
> *make yourselves holy! Straightway the whole*
>   *land shall dance,*
> *whenever Bromios leads his bands*   115
> *to the mountain, the mountain; where awaits*

---

find "the bacchic branch" waved like a thyrsus at 308 and maenads putting on garlands of oak, as well as of ivy and milax or bryony, at 703. Since milax (for which bryony is given as a conventional equivalent; at any rate it is a rampant, berried evergreen) is mentioned in this context also, at 108, there is something to be said for the garland interpretation. Fir is added to oak because the two trees go together, particularly in this play; they do of course grow on mountains, including Cithaeron. They are stressed, perhaps, because DIONYSUS was associated with trees as well as with ivy, vines, goats, bulls, snakes, and lions; in some places he was worshipped as *Dendrítēs*, "of the trees."

111– Fawnskins are ritual bacchic apparel, described as "sacred" at
113 137. The fawn has the speed and freedom emulated by the mountain dancers, and Dodds rightly compares the fawn simile at 866ff. The skins are to be in some way "garlanded" (as the verb means literally, rather than "fringed") with white wool— either by winding it around the belt, by forming a belt itself, or more probably by adding a fringe of short lengths of wool around the bottom of the skin to form a sort of circle or garland. Woollen fillets or headbands were used in other cults to signify the consecration of the worshipper.

115 There is an important doubt about the text here. It is defective in the word translated "whenever"; the two manuscripts give a simple but unmetrical (and in the present context ungrammatical) word meaning "when" (*hot*'). The possible alternatives, of which I prefer and translate the second, are to restore a somewhat similar-looking word meaning "whoever" (*hostis*) or to restore a less familiar word for "when," adding the indefinite

the female throng,
away from looms and from shuttles
stung to madness by Dionysus.

ANTISTROPHE 2

O lair of the Couretes,   120
sacred haunts of Crete

---

particle to fit syntax and metre and give the sense "whenever"
(*eut' an*).

The difference in resulting sense is significant. If *"whoever*
leads the bands is Bromios"* (that is, DIONYSUS), then the
CHORUS is asserting that any human leader actually becomes
the god as a result of his exaltation—a very remarkable idea.
"Whenever" gives a less startling sense and a better sequence
of thought: the whole land will dance whenever DIONYSUS
leads his band to the mountain. Here the god is envisaged as
the real leader, as indeed will be stated at 140. Later in the ode,
but not necessarily here, he is imagined as taking part in the
dances himself (see note on 145).

120ff On the story of the birth of Zeus in Crete (which was famous
for its sacred caves; cf. 123) and on Euripides' syncretistic tendencies, see also the notes on 58f. and 78–82. The Cretan Couretes are here called Corybantes (why they are "triple-helmeted"
is unclear), who were actually Asiatic demons associated with
Cybele, to whom the wild music of drum and flute originally
belonged. The mention of "bacchic dance" in 126 is strictly
inappropriate to the cult of Rhea in Crete, unless it is a purely
generic term here. Formally the transition to DIONYSUS is man-
aged by the introduction of the Satyrs in 130. They were creatures with the tail, hooves, and ears of a horse (later a goat)
who became associated with DIONYSUS, and they accompanied
him, according to legend, when he was driven mad by a jealous
Hera; they probably cured him by the noise of the drum, which
was believed to have this property. The allusion is oblique, but
the audience would know the mythology of DIONYSUS particularly well (pp. 2f.); and the Satyrs were closely connected with
the tragic festivals.

> which gave birth to Zeus,
> where, triple-helmeted in their cave,
> this circle of stretched hide
> the Corybantes invented for me;   125
> and in tense bacchic dance
> they blended the drum with sweet-crying
> breath
> of Phrygian flutes, and into mother Rhea's
> hand they placed it, a beat for the bacchants'
> cries.

> From her the ecstatic Satyrs   130
> obtained it, from the mother-goddess,
> and joined it to the dances
> of the festival each second year
> in which Dionysus rejoices.

EPODE

> Well-pleasing in the mountains he, who from
> the running bands   135
> falls to the ground, wearing

---

133 Since DIONYSUS' main orgiastic festival took place in historical
times in midwinter and only every second year, it cannot have
been a typical fertility or dying-and-reborn-god cult, which
would be annual and in the early spring. The evidence, mainly
from inscriptions, is cited by Dodds, *The Greeks and the Irrational*, p. 278, n. 2.

135ff Another textual difficulty, analogous to that at 115: what is
the exact meaning of the word translated "well-pleasing," and
to whom does it refer? The Greek word (*hēdus*) means "pleasant," "sweet" (but *not* "joyful," at this period). Moreover the
translation "who from the running bands" involves a change,
though only of a single letter, from the reading of the manuscripts, which means "*when* from." If we keep strictly to that
reading, then the subject of the sentence must be DIONYSUS,

> *the sacred cloak of fawnskin, hunting*   137
> *goat-slain blood, the joy of eating raw flesh,*
>   *speeding*
> *to the mountains of Phrygia, of Lydia, and the* 140

---

who is sweet to (that is, in the eyes of) his worshippers; the difficulty here is "and the leader is Bromios" in 141. Even if we
give "and" the force of "for," the statement is still redundant
and a little odd. If we accept the change of "when" to "who"
in 135, then the god, who is the over-all leader or inspirer of
the worship (note on 115), is pleased when a worshipper falls to
the ground and eats raw flesh in a climax of ecstasy.

The choice is important, and it depends in part on a minute
assessment of the Greek and of the accuracy of transmission of
the text. If we make DIONYSUS the subject, then we must envisage *him* as devouring raw flesh, as fulfilling the key role in his
own rites. I find this improbable (even though DIONYSUS is mentioned shortly before, at 134); I think his mention at 141 is a
real difficulty to this view; and·I believe the CHORUS is still
thinking of the god, at this point, as the unseen leader and
motivator of the dances, as at 115. At 142 the tone of the ode
changes, and miracles begin—the ground flows with milk, wine,
and honey. Now, and now only, is the god imagined as appearing in the flesh to urge on his worshippers, from 144 to the end
of the ode: a climax to the epode and the whole song, but not
really so if the god has already been eating raw flesh at 138f.
But the question is much disputed.

138f *goat-slain blood, the joy of eating raw flesh:* the tearing-to-pieces
(*sparagmos*) and eating raw (*ōmophagia*) of an animal—goat,
fawn, or bull—was a ritual element in Dionysiac worship, as is
confirmed by later inscriptions and comments in later writers.
The purpose, as has already been stressed, was probably to bring
the worshipper as close as possible to the life, power, and libera-
tion of wild Nature, which DIONYSUS represented. The dancer
falls to the ground either in a kind of seizure of inspiration or
in order to grasp and tear the animal victim. (Dodds' objection

> *leader is Bromios, euoi!*
> *The ground flows with milk, flows with wine,*
> *flows with bees' nectar.*
> *Like the smoke of Syrian frankincense*
> *the Bacchic god holding high*   **145**
> *the fiery flame of the pine torch*
> *streams it from his rod,*
> *with running and dances*
> *rousing the stragglers,*
> *swinging them on with cries of ecstasy*
> *and tossing his luxuriant locks in the air.*   **150**

---

to the latter motive, based on the present tense of "hunting," that the animal has not yet been caught, seems ill-founded.) The imagined dancer is a male, but there is no reason for doubting that the female maenads, who formed the bulk of DIONYSUS' followers, joined in the tearing-to-pieces—as AGAUE and the Theban women certainly do later in the play—and also in the eating of the raw flesh which logically followed, as AGAUE seems to invite the CHORUS to share in eating what she believes to be a lion's head at 1184.

141 *euoi* represents a cry of ecstasy and invocation used in the cult of DIONYSUS and no other god.

145 The term translated as *Bacchic god* is *Bakcheus* in Greek; in its few other uses in drama it refers to DIONYSUS, as does *Bakchios,* and not to his worshippers, who are *Bakchoi* or *Bakchai* (as at 129, 152). The point is important: it is the god himself who is described as rallying his followers and addressing them and holding the torch aloft. This receives confirmation from the mention of "luxuriant locks" in 150—compare 235, 455, where DIONYSUS (the Lydian stranger) is similarly described; and from 557f., where the god leads with the thyrsus his sacred bands.

147 *streams it from his rod:* "rod" normally refers to the thyrsus, but here, I think, it must refer to the torch—though some interpreters have taken the words in a different way.

Among the joyful cries he makes these
words roar out:
"O *onward bacchants,*
onward bacchants!
Ornamented with gold of Tmolus' river
to the deep beat of the drums   156
sing and dance to Dionysus   155
exalting the god to whom you cry in ecstasy
amid Phrygian cries and incantations
when the holy melodious flute   160
sounds out its holy uplifting strains,
accompanying
you on your way to the mountain, the
mountain." *Joyfully*   165
then, as a foal with its grazing mother,
the bacchant springs around with nimble feet.

Enter TIRESIAS.

TIRESIAS Who is at the gate? Call out Cadmus from the
palace—   170

---

154 Literally, "with luxury of gold-flowing Tmolus"—the reference
is to the gold-bearing river Pactolus, which like Mount Tmolus
is in Lydia (see note on 13–19). The meaning is probably that
these Lydian bacchants are wearing gold ornaments, rather than
that their instruments are golden, or that "luxury" is a vocative
and addressed figuratively to the women themselves.

157f *in ecstasy*: literally, "to whom you cry *'euoi.'* " See note on 141.

166 *as a foal*: a similar comparison to a "fawn playing in the green
pleasures of a meadow" occurs in a later choral ode at 862ff.
The foal and the fawn symbolize freedom, gracefulness, relaxation, and closeness to Nature—but also, in the case of the
fawn, vulnerability.

170– *Scene 1, 170–369* (a scene or "episode," to use the technical
369 term taken from Greek, is a sequence of action marked off by a
formal ode at its beginning and end). DIONYSUS has gone to
Cithaeron, and the CHORUS has described the joys of his wor-

43

Agenor's son, who left the Sidonian land
and fortified this town of the Thebans.
Go, someone, announce that Tiresias
is looking for him; he knows why I have come—
the agreement that I made with him, an old man with his elder: 175
to fit up thyrsi and wear the skins of fawns
and crown our heads with shoots of ivy.

    Enter CADMUS.

CADMUS   Dearest friend—for I listened and heard your voice,

---

ship. Now two old men, CADMUS and the seer TIRESIAS (a recurrent figure in the Theban saga), exemplify some of the wrong reasons for taking up the new religion and then allow PENTHEUS, at his very first appearance, to display the worst side of his nature.

There is an element of charade in the aged pair of bacchants, but it should not be exaggerated by the contention that the whole of this part of the scene is burlesque. A more important question is why Euripides assigns such a prominent position to the display of false reasons (upholding the family reputation; exaggerating DIONYSUS' effects in a quasi-philosophical manner) for the new religion. Partly, no doubt, it is to emphasize the ambiguity of the cult and to exemplify once again, as Euripides enjoyed doing, the frequent alliance between religion and hypocrisy; but mainly he is setting out a consciously rhetorical statement of the case for and against DIONYSUS, in which many of the possible arguments, both good and bad, are formally marshalled in a manner that strikes us as frigid but that suited the intellectual climate of late fifth-century Athens, sophist- and demagogue-ridden, war-weary, and thick with new insights into logic and language.

171f   It was customary in drama to supply stage directions by identifying each new character by his place of origin and his family as he came on the scene. According to myth CADMUS had come to Greece from Sidon in Phoenicia in search of his sister Europa, who had been abducted by Zeus, and he founded Thebes in obedience to an oracle from Apollo at Delphi.

a wise voice from a wise man, as I was in the house:
here I am, quite ready, with all this apparatus of the god—   180
for since he is the child of my daughter's womb   181
we must magnify him and make him as important as we can.   183
Where must we go to dance, in which direction turn our feet
and set our grey heads tossing? Expound this to me,   185
one old man to another, Tiresias, for you are wise;
because I should not tire, all night or all day long,
of striking the earth with the thyrsus. We have joyfully forgotten
that we are old!

TIRESIAS   You experience the same as I do, then;
for I too feel like a stripling and shall undertake the dances.   190

CADMUS   Shall we then journey to the mountain by chariot?

---

179   The first mention of a word—*sophos*, meaning wise, expe-
rienced, intelligent in a sophisticated way, or clever—that is of
great significance in this play, and that is used to oppose pretentious intellectualism to the simpler wisdom of obeying the
gods and following Nature. TIRESIAS, as a seer and prophet and
interpreter of omens, should be *sophos* in more than the least
sense, but he turns out not to be so; his friend CADMUS obviously admires him greatly. On *sophos* compare 30, 186, 200,
203, 266, 395 and note, 480 and note, 641 and note, 655f. and
note, 824 and note, 839, 877 and note, 1151 and note, 1190.

186–   It is repeatedly emphasized that DIONYSUS enables his wor-
190   shippers to transcend their usual physical limitations, to do things
without labour or with only a slight effort that is not wearisome
but pure joy. The two old men seem to share in the feeling of
lightness, even if they follow the god for the wrong reasons.
Incidentally, have they been deliberately infatuated by DIO-
NYSUS, or do they alone of the men of Thebes (195f.) freely
choose to follow him for the reasons they describe? This is not
made clear either here or in CADMUS' reappearance at the end
of the play—where, however, he is a dignified figure (cf. note
on 1360–62).

191–   This is the first occurrence in the play of *stichomythia*, or a
199   conversation in alternating single-verse utterances. It was a con-

45

TIRESIAS   No— the god would not have equal honour, so.

CADMUS   Shall I guide you like a child, though both of us are old?

TIRESIAS   The god will lead us there without toil.

CADMUS   And shall we be the only men in the land to dance for the bacchic god?   195

TIRESIAS   Yes, for only we are sane—the rest are mad.

CADMUS   We are wasting time; take hold of my hand.

TIRESIAS   There, clasp mine and make it a pair.

CADMUS   I am a mortal, and do not despise the gods.

TIRESIAS   Our wisdom is as nothing in the eyes of deity.   200
The traditions of our fathers, from time immemorial
our possession—no argument casts them down,
not even by the wisest invention of the keenest mind.
Will it be said that I have no shame for old age

---

ventional form in tragedy, often used to convey excitement. That this is the case here is confirmed by the excited division of a verse between speakers at 189, a relatively uncommon event. In more extended passages of stichomythia, as for example between DIONYSUS and PENTHEUS at 463–508, the purpose is rather eristic or controversial, to provide a precise, formal, and forceful confrontation between two opposed points of view. The brevity of each statement often leads to an intentional ambiguity, to misunderstandings, and to the division of a single thought between two or three verses in which each speaker interrupts or caps the other.

200ff TIRESIAS' professions of conservatism are odd for one who goes on to demonstrate sophistic cleverness and rationalism at its worst. He is part hypocritical, part confused: *The traditions of our fathers* clearly do not have much bearing on strange new cults like that of DIONYSUS, though the CHORUS, too, likes to stress the traditional affiliations of its god.

since I intend to crown my head with ivy and to dance?   205
But the god has made no distinction, whether it is the young
who must dance or the older man,
but he wishes to have honours equally from all,
counting no one apart in his desire to be magnified.

    CADMUS   Since, Tiresias, you do not see this daylight here   210
I shall become your interpreter of events by words:
Pentheus approaches, hurrying toward this house,
Echion's son, to whom I have given the power over this land.
How excited he is! Whatever news will he recount?

    PENTHEUS   I chanced to be away from this land,   215
but hear of the evils that have just broken out in the
    city—
that our women have abandoned their homes
in fake bacchic revels, and in the deep-shaded
mountains are roaming around, honouring with dances
the new-made god Dionysus, whoever he is;   220
that wine-bowls are set among the sacred companies

---

210   TIRESIAS is traditionally blind. "Seeing the daylight" is standard
tragic language for (1) being alive or (2) being able to see.

215ff PENTHEUS indulges in what amounts to a soliloquy, for he does
not see the old men until 248 and he would scarcely be addressing the CHORUS of foreign bacchants.

221– It is an important part of PENTHEUS' character that he con-
225   tinually harps on drunkenness and immorality as characteristic
of the new cult. Both charges are false, as DIONYSUS will state
and as the MESSENGERS from Cithaeron, as well as the CHORUS,
will confirm. PENTHEUS, in fact, appears to have a special and
personal preoccupation with sex—as is suggested by the gloating
tone of 222f.—which could hardly be grounded in the facts
about the Dionysiac cult that Euripides chooses to present.
Admittedly the orgiastic cults in general had by this time
acquired something of a reputation for drunkenness; and in
Euripides' Ion, for instance, it seemed quite natural for Ion's
father to confess that he had engendered him during a Bacchic

full to the brim, and that one by one the women go crouching
into the wilderness, to serve the lechery of men—
they profess to be maenads making sacrifice,
but actually they put Aphrodite before the Bacchic god.   225
As many as I have caught, with their hands in chains
warders are guarding in the public prisons;
but all who are at large I shall hunt from the mountain,   228
shall fasten them down in iron nets   231
and put a quick end to this villainous bacchic rite.
    It is said that some stranger has arrived,
a wizard and enchanter from the Lydian land,
his hair all fragrant with light-brown tresses,   235
with ruddy cheeks and the charms of Aphrodite in his eyes,
who daylong and nightlong mingles with young girls
holding out before them his rituals of holy joy.
But if I catch him within these walls
I shall put a stop to his beating of the thyrsus and tossing   240
of his locks, by cutting his neck clean off from his body.
That is the fellow who asserts that Dionysus is a god
and was once sewn in the thigh of Zeus—
the child who in fact was burnt up by the lightning's flame
together with his mother, because she had lied about Zeus being
        her lover.   245
Does not this deserve the dreaded noose,
behaving in this outrageous way, whoever the stranger may be?
    But here is another miracle! I see the diviner
Tiresias in dappled fawnskins,

---

celebration at Delphi. Yet PENTHEUS' attitude exceeds by far
what would be required for the mere representation of popular
opinion.

235– The same malicious and perhaps morbid attitude is shown by
238 PENTHEUS' implication that DIONYSUS is a professional seducer
     and by the suggestive ambiguity of "mingles" in 237 and "hold-
     ing out [literally, 'stretching forth'] . . . his rituals" in 238.

243– See note on 96ff.; here of course PENTHEUS adopts the sceptical
245 explanation of Semele's punishment.

and my mother's father making himself ridiculous, 250
playing the bacchant with a thyrsus-rod. I am ashamed, old man,
to see the foolish senility of the pair of you.
Will you not shake off the ivy this minute? Let free
your hand from the thyrsus, grandfather!
It is you, Tiresias, who have persuaded him to this; once again
    you want— 255
by introducing this new deity to mankind—
to have more birds to watch, more fees from burnt offerings!
If your grey old age did not preserve you,
you would be sitting in chains in the midst of the bacchants
for introducing pernicious rites—for where women 260
have the sparkle of the vine in their festivities,
there, I say, nothing wholesome remains in their rituals.

CHORUS   Impiety! Foreigner, do you not reverence the gods
and Cadmus, who sowed the earth-born crop?
You are Echion's child—do you want to shame his family? 265

TIRESIAS   When a wise man chooses a sane basis

260– PENTHEUS' insinuation that the bacchants get drunk is contra-
262 dicted by the first MESSENGER's report (686–88) of the utterly
sober demeanour of the Theban women on Cithaeron. Neither
TIRESIAS (278ff.) nor indeed the CHORUS itself (e.g., 381–86)
will attempt to deny that DIONYSUS' gift of wine is a great benefit to mankind, and the first MESSENGER, expressing his own
views, goes so far as to link wine and love (771–74); but drunkenness has no part in the mountain rituals of the bacchants—
that at least is the idea propagated in this play. See also pages
4f.

265 PENTHEUS' mother AGAUE married Echion, one of the "earth-
born" warriors who grew from CADMUS' sowing of the dragon's
teeth when he founded Thebes. So PENTHEUS had a special
reason for defending the family honour.

266– The contrast between the glib and the honest speaker, the blus-
271 terer and the man of sense, good premises for an argument and
bad ones, was of particular interest for Athenians, both because

for his arguments, it is no great task to speak well;
but you have a glib tongue, as though in your right mind,
yet in your words there is no real sense.
The man who is influential by sheer aggressiveness, and knows
    how to speak,   270
proves to be a bad citizen—for he lacks sanity.
    This new god, whom you deride—
I could not describe how great
he will be throughout Hellas. For there are two things, young
    man,

---

of contemporary speculations about the nature of rhetoric and
the capacity of sophists to teach it and because of some painful
examples, in the course of the Peloponnesian War, of the gap
between political persuasiveness and political reality.

274– Tiresias' arguments against Pentheus and for Dionysus may
318 be summarized as follows:

1. Demeter (an acknowledged deity) and Dionysus cover the
   twin spheres of solid and liquid nourishment respectively.
2. Wine, the gift of Dionysus, soothes pain, brings sleep; also
   it is poured as a libation to other gods and so produces other
   benefits.
3. The theory of Dionysus being sewn in the thigh of Zeus is
   indeed far-fetched but arises from an etymological confusion.
4. As bringer of frenzy and inspiration Dionysus is associated
   with prophecy and panic, both commonly regarded as divine
   in origin.
5. If women are occasionally immoral, that is not because of
   Dionysus but because of their own lack of chastity.

Some of these arguments are arid, and are probably meant to
be so.

274– The force of this argument is that dry and liquid nourishment
280 are opposed and complementary; Demeter is responsible for the
former and is an unquestioned goddess; therefore Dionysus too
must be a god. The attachment of gods to natural products
seems to have been stressed by the sophist Prodicus, and the
opposition of wet and dry (as well as of hot and cold) was a
commonplace of archaic Greek thought.

that are first among humans: the goddess Demeter   275
(she is the earth; call her which name you like)—
she nourishes men by way of dry food;
and he who filled the complementary role, Semele's offspring,
discovered the grape-cluster's liquid drink and introduced it
to mortals, that which stops wretched men   280
from suffering, when they are filled with the stream of the vine,
and gives sleep as oblivion of the evils that happen by day;
nor is there any other cure against distress.
He is poured as a libation to the gods, a god himself,
so it is through him that men have all good things.   285
Another point: you laugh at him and the story of his being sewn
        into Zeus'
thigh? I will teach you how subtle this really is.
When Zeus had snatched him from the lightning's fire
and brought the baby to Olympus as a god,
Hera wanted to hurl it out of heaven;   290
but Zeus devised a counterscheme in a truly divine fashion:
he broke off a portion of the ether that encircles
the earth, and made this into a "hostage" which he handed over

    •   •   •   •   •   •

[and so saved]

Dionysus from Hera's hostility. So in time
men say he was sewn in the "thigh" of Zeus,   295
making up the story once they had changed the word,
because he had been "hostage" to Hera, god to goddess.
    He is a prophet, too, this deity; since that which is bacchic
and that which is manic possesses great mantic powers;

292f TIRESIAS' apparently feeble explanation depends on the similar-
      ity of the Greek word for hostage, _homēros_, with that for thigh,
      mēros (and also, probably, with that for portion, _měros_, in 292);
      see note on 367. The making of doubles and the hostility of
      Hera to her husband's human mistresses and offspring are
      common themes of myth, the former also exemplified at 629f.
299   The connection of Dionysiac madness with prophecy depends
      mainly on the similarity of their names, closely represented by

for whenever the god enters the body in full spate   300
he makes those who are maddened tell the future.
And he partakes of Ares, has a certain share of him;
for an army under arms and in full military order
is scattered by terror before it lays hands on a lance.
This too is a madness sent from Dionysus.   305
In time to come you shall see him even on the Delphic cliffs
leaping with pine torches over the twin-peaked plateau,
swinging and brandishing the bacchic branch,
and great through all Hellas. But obey me, Pentheus:
do not be too confident that sovereignty is what rules men;   310
nor, if you hold an opinion, but your judgment is sick,
take that opinion for good sense. Receive the god into this land
and pour offerings, and be a bacchant, and garland your head.
It is not Dionysus who will force women to be virtuous

     "manic" and "mantic" in English, though the two terms may in fact be related in origin. In actual practice DIONYSUS had only slight associations with prophecy, which belonged to Apollo; similarly with warfare (which belonged to Ares) and panic in battle (associated with Pan). Yet from a theoretical point of view TIRESIAS was justified in claiming a share in these definitely divine manifestations, since DIONYSUS' quality of producing frenzy in his worshipers does have a general connection with them.

306f   DIONYSUS did of course gain a foothold at Delphi and was believed in historical times to occupy the shrine beneath the "twin-peaked plateau" (the peaks being the pair of "shining rocks," the Phaedriades, which overhang the sanctuary) for the three winter months of each year when Apollo was absent. In a well-known passage of Plutarch (*Moralia* 953 D), we learn that the maenads of his day were almost stranded on Mount Parnassus in a snowstorm.

314– This answer to PENTHEUS' sneers at 221f. again reflects current
318   preoccupations with *physis*, natural quality, as against the humanly ordered environment. Its place in TIRESIAS' argument is a little artificial, and there may be some disarray in the text

in the realm of Cypris, but one must watch for this   315
in their own nature; for even amid bacchic celebrations   317
the woman who is truly virtuous will not be corrupted.
    You see how you are pleased, when the multitude
throngs the palace doors, and the city magnifies the name of
      Pentheus;   320
so Dionysus too, in my opinion, delights in being honoured.
Therefore I and Cadmus, whom you make fun of,
shall crown ourselves with ivy and shall dance—
a grey-haired couple, but all the same dance we must;
and I refuse to be persuaded by your arguments into fighting
      against a god;   325
for you are most grievously mad—beyond the cure
of drugs, and yet your sickness must be due to them.

CHORUS   Old man, your words bring no shame on Phoebus,
and in honouring Bromios, a mighty god, you show good sense.

CADMUS   My son, Tiresias exhorted you well;   330
dwell with us, not outside the accustomed ways.
For at present your mind has taken wing, and your thought is
    no thought.
Even if this is no god, as you assert,
let him be called one by you—tell a lie in a good cause,

---

here—unless TIRESIAS is crowding in, somewhat out of their
logical order, all the remaining arguments he can think of.

315 *Cypris:* Aphrodite, who had an ancient and important cult at
Paphos in Cyprus.

326f PENTHEUS is like a snake that feeds its venom on evil drugs, as
at *Iliad* 22. 94, and his madness is so great that drugs like helle-
bore, the traditional specific, would be needed to cure it. The
antithesis is a little forced, and many critics have thought the
text slightly corrupt.

328f Such harmless, often almost pointless, comments by the
CHORUS are in the established tragic tradition, in which the
chorus usually represent moderate opinion and express it in
very conventional terms. Certainly choruses are rarely clever.

that he is Semele's child, so that it may seem that she bore a
    god   335
and we gain honour for all our family.
You see the miserable fate of Actaeon,
whom the carnivorous hounds he reared
tore apart, when he boasted that he was better
at hunting than Artemis in the mountain glens.   340
Do not suffer a similar fate! Come here, let me crown your head
with ivy; in company with us give honour to the god.

    PENTHEUS Keep your hands off me—go and perform your
      bacchic rites
and don't wipe off your foolishness on me!
Tiresias here, the instructor of your folly,   345
I shall punish. Go, someone, with all speed,
and when you come to his throne where he takes the omens,
prise it with levers and turn it upside down;
mix everything up in utter confusion,

337– Actaeon was CADMUS' dead grandson and is mentioned on two
340 other occasions in the play (at 1227 and 1291, 230 being probably an interpolation), clearly because he, like PENTHEUS, suffered a kind of *sparagmos* or tearing-to-pieces on Cithaeron—
by his own hounds, who are described at 338 as "carnivorous"
or "eaters of raw food," reminding one of the "joy of eating raw
flesh" of 139. Other versions of Actaeon's offence were known
in the classical period; but the punishment of a mortal for
boasting that he can surpass a god is an old theme, as is the
nature of his punishment here.

346– There is a kind of spitefulness, a total lack of magnanimity, in
351 PENTHEUS' proposed punishment of TIRESIAS and in the deliberate and complacent way in which he outlines it. This young
man (he *is* young, we must remember, as is confirmed for example by 974 and by his mother's mad words at 1185–87) is
developing early some of the worst qualities of the tyrant, and it
is inconceivable to me (although it has not been so to a few
commentators in the past) that Euripides does not mean his
audience to realize it.

and fling his sacred fillets to the winds and storms: 350
by doing this I shall pain him most!
The rest of you go through the city and track down
the effeminate stranger, who is introducing a new disease
for our women and dishonouring their beds.
And if you catch him, lead him here   355
in chains to get his deserts by stoning
and so die, after seeing a bitter end to bacchanals in Thebes.

TIRESIAS Wretched man, how ignorant you are of what you
     are saying!
Before, you were out of your mind—but now you are raving
     mad.
Let us be on our way, Cadmus, and beseech the god   360
for this man's sake, wild though he is,
and for the city's, to do nothing drastic.
But follow me with your ivy staff
and try to support my body, as I will yours.
It is shameful for two old men to fall. Yet so be it,   365
since we must serve the Bacchic god, the son of Zeus.
Let Pentheus see that he brings no mourning upon

353f Again the sexual preoccupation, almost obsession; see note on
      221–25.

356f Stoning to death was one of the special punishments for sac-
      rilege.

358– TIRESIAS' ignoring of the impending destruction of his oracular
362   seat may be a dramatic simplification (or it may imply that he
      knew by his prophetic gifts that it would not in fact be dam-
      aged—at least, for what this is worth, it was displayed by
      Theban guides centuries later, according to Pausanias). Even
      apart from this, his reply to PENTHEUS seems to show a genuine
      forbearance which makes PENTHEUS' behaviour even more odious.

364– The vigour of Dionysiac inspiration is pathetically gone—be-
366   cause of the depressing encounter with PENTHEUS, or because
      the first flush of self-delusion has died away?

367   The Greek for "mourning" is *penthos*, and the obvious pun on

your house, Cadmus. *It is not by prophecy that I say this,*
but by the facts—for he who speaks folly is himself a fool.
  Exeunt CADMUS and TIRESIAS.

STROPHE 1

CHORUS   Holiness, queen among gods,   370

PENTHEUS' name is much emphasized in this play; cf. 508, 1113.
The idea that there was a significant relationship between name
and object was a familiar one, accepted for example by Heraclitus of Ephesus and still discussed by Plato in his *Cratylus.*
Aeschylus was particularly fond of such significant puns. See
also the note on 299.

370– The *First Stasimon*, or first "stationary" ode (which does not
432   imply that the CHORUS did not dance to it, only that they
did not proceed into or out of the orchestra during it), consists
simply of two strophic pairs. The first is in predominantly Ionic
metre (note on 64ff.), which is more obviously appropriate to the
indignant invocation of the earlier verses than to the more reflective content of what follows; the second pair is predominantly Aeolic. The opening strophe calls on Holiness to witness
PENTHEUS' sacrilegious insolence to DIONYSUS, who is described
as a harmless god who presides over feasting, wine, and gaiety.
Its antistrophe stresses the advantages of a quiet life over law-
lessness and folly, which the gods detect from afar. In the
second strophe the CHORUS longs to escape to Cyprus, island of
Aphrodite and of Love, or to Pieria where the Muses dwell—
peaceful and beautiful places where bacchants might be free to
conduct their rites. The second antistrophe further describes
the gaiety and peace brought by the god and associates him with
the idea of a moderate, restrained, and unspectacular life.

  The tone is in general firm, calm, and reflective, but the ode
is punctuated by brief passages of veiled threat. There is more
to it, and to the CHORUS' state of mind, than meets the eye. The
simple and clear philosophy of life, the relaxed and lyrical
evocation of Cyprus and Pieria, of peace and feasting, become

Holiness, who over earth
carry your golden wing,
do you hear these words of Pentheus?
Do you hear his unholy
insolence to Bromios, the son   375
of Semele, he who amid fair-
garlanded feastings is fore-
most divinity of the blessed ones? These are his gifts:
dancing in the sacred band
and laughing as the flute plays   380
and putting an end to cares
whenever the grape-cluster's gleam
comes in the feast of the gods, and in the ivy-

---

slightly sinister when one remembers what these women are suppressing—all the violent side of Dionysus' worship, for which they live. It is a totally different picture of the god from that of the preceding ode, and not simply because Euripides may be describing, for a change, the emasculated worship and more harmless Dionysiac associations of his own time and city. Of course Pentheus represents insolence and violence, and the quieter aspects of the god he rejects are emphasized to point up his folly; but that does not seem to be the whole explanation.

370 *Holiness* (or perhaps one should call it "Reverence"—at least it is a quality of mind that determines one's actions to the gods as well as to men) is a free personification, unestablished by tradition or cult, and distinct, for example, from the Graces (in 414) in this respect. Describing Holiness as "queen of the gods" and as having wings of gold is a poetical device, in which the use of the traditional phraseology of worship is designed to give substance to what is little more than an abstract antithesis of Pentheus' "unholy insolence" at 374f. Later in the play the similar personification of bloody Vengeance (in the refrain of the Fourth Stasimon at 991 and 1011) stands in antiphonal contrast. Other personifications in this ode add to the tone of simple philosophizing; so of the Loves, Desire, Peace.

383 *feast of the gods:* an epic phrase, as Dodds observes—the feast

bearing festivities the mixing-
bowl casts sleep   385
over men.

ANTISTROPHE 1

Of unbridled mouths   386
and lawless folly
the result is misfortune;
but the peaceful life
and sanity   390
remain unshaken and
hold the house together; for far away
though they dwell in the upper air
the heavenly ones behold the affairs of men.
Cleverness is not wisdom,   395
nor is thinking thoughts that are not mortal.
Life is short; this being so,
who would pursue great things
and not bear with what is at hand? These
are the ways of madmen and   400
men of evil counsel, at least
in my judgment.

STROPHE 2

O that I might come to Cyprus,   402

---

is a human one, but libations to the gods would be constantly
poured, and so it becomes also divine.

385 *mixing-bowl*: the Greeks drank their wine mixed with water
(usually two parts water to one wine), and the mixture stood
in a wide bowl from which the cups were filled.

395 *cleverness . . . wisdom*: the words are different forms of
sophos (note on 179), and the meaning is that "the excessively
wise does not constitute true wisdom."

402– The CHORUS in their wishes for escape are treated as Greeks
416 rather than as foreigners; they think of Cyprus because it

Aphrodite's island,
where the Loves range, beguilers
   of the minds of mortals;
and to Paphos, which the hundred-mouthed   406
streams of the alien river
   make fruitful, fed by no rain!
Or, where is lovely
Pieria, the Muses' haunt,   410
   revered slope of Olympus,
thither bring me, Bromios, Bromios,
   god who leads the bacchic adoration!
     There are the Graces
     and there Desire; and there for bacchants   415
   it is lawful to hold their rites.

ANTISTROPHE 2

The god who is child of Zeus
   rejoices in festivities
and loves Peace, giver of
   prosperity, goddess who rears young men.   420

---

was, for Greeks, the birthplace of Aphrodite, goddess of love and reconciliation, who was also occasionally associated with Dionysus in cult—perhaps because of the fertility aspects of each. But both here and in the unusual association of Pieria, the home of the Muses, with Desire, sexual love is used to symbolize freedom and peace.

407f The alien river fed by no rain is obviously the Nile, and there must have been a story (otherwise unattested) that it ran under the sea and came up in Cyprus, just as the Alpheius was imagined as coming up in Syracuse.

410 Pieria, birthplace of the Muses, is a region of pleasant rivers and valleys to the north of Mount Olympus; again it is an obvious symbol of relaxation and happiness and one that will be especially associated with Dionysus at 565f. It is not so remote as Cyprus but is close to Euripides' own place of retreat in Macedonia.

In equal shares, both to the prosperous
and to the lesser man, he has given possession
of wine's joy that keeps out grief.
He hates the man who has no care for this:
by day and by pleasant nights   425
to live out a life of contentment.
It is wise to withhold one's heart and mind
from men who think themselves superior.
Whatever the multitude,   430
the ordinary people, take as normal and
practise, this would I accept.   433

SERVANT   See, Pentheus, we have hunted down this quarry

433–   *Scene 2, 433–518:* The disguised DIONYSUS is led in by a
518   SERVANT, who describes (quite briefly, but with some of the
       grandiloquence typical of messengers in tragedy) his docility
       and, the first of the strange happenings in Thebes, the escape
       of the women. PENTHEUS ignores this information and its im-
       plications and concentrates on an aggressive interrogation of
       the stranger, in a long stichomythia (note on 191–99) in which
       each of his jibes is countered or turned against him. (This inter-
       rogation perhaps had a prototype in the questioning by Lycur-
       gus in Aeschylus' *Edonians.*) At the end of the scene the god
       allows himself to be led away, as he had been led in at its
       beginning. This is the first of a balanced sequence of three
       scenes (see also notes on 576–861 and 912–76) that disclose
       PENTHEUS' degradation from apparent domination to being
       DIONYSUS' infatuated and absurd creature, with a corresponding
       revelation by the god of his own true power and nature.

434ff The SERVANT has carried out PENTHEUS' orders (at 352–56) for
       the stranger's arrest, presumably near Cithaeron (62f.), and
       reports what happened and what did not. It was a necessary
       convention of the Greek theatre that distant, violent, or com-
       plex actions took place offstage and were then described by a
       messenger. The messenger-speech is an important element of
       Greek tragedy, and its expression, often rather artificial, was

60

against whom you sent us, and our endeavour was not in vain.   435
This beast, we found, was gentle, and did not take
to flight, but proffered his hands quite willingly;
he did not turn pale, his cheeks did not change their ruddy hue,
but smiling he invited me both to bind him and take him away,
and stood still, making things easy for me.   440
And I, feeling ashamed, said to him: "Stranger, not of my choice
do I lead you off, but by the orders of Pentheus who sent me."
But as for the bacchants you locked up, put under mass arrest
and bound in the chains of the public jail—
they are gone, those women, released, and to the mountain
     glens   445
they are dancing their way, calling on Bromios as their god.
Of themselves the chains came undone from their feet,
and the doors were unbarred without mortal hand.
Full of many wonders this man has come
to our city of Thebes—but the rest is your concern.   450

PENTHEUS   Let go of his hands—he is in my net
and cannot escape me, however swift he is.
Well, stranger, you are not unshapely in your body,

---

worked out with particular care. The present report is only a
short sample of the genre; two full-length speeches, describing
subsequent events on Cithaeron, will come later.

436   *beast:* continues the "quarry" metaphor of 434, but is significant in the light of PENTHEUS' delusion at 618ff. and 920ff. that
the stranger is a bull.

439   The stranger's graceful and sinister smile is no doubt fixed by
the actor's mask. The same smile belongs to the god in his
undisguised form, and at 1021 the CHORUS prays to him to cast
his noose "with smiling face." It was a traditional feature, as is
shown by the *Homeric Hymn to Dionysus*, VII, 14, where the
god sits smiling when he is captured by pirates. His relaxed and
pleased demeanor emphasizes his divine confidence and im-
perturbability, his indifference to human concerns as such, and
his embodiment of youthful grace and vigour.

so far as women are concerned—and it is for this that you are
    here in Thebes.
Your locks are long, through keeping clear of wrestling,   455
and flow right down by your cheeks, full of desire;
and you keep your complexion fair by careful contrivance—
not in the sun's rays, but under the shade
hunting the pleasures of Aphrodite with your beauty.
Now first tell me who you are, what is your family.   460

   Dionysus (Lydian Stranger)   I do not hesitate to do so; it is
    easy to tell.
You must know by hearsay of flowery Tmolus.

   Pentheus   I know, the range that rings the town of Sardis.

   Dionysus   I am from there, and Lydia is my native land.

455–
459

The *Homeric Hymn* cited in the preceding note, and composed probably in the sixth century B.C., also mentions (at
line 4) the god's long hair—which is incompatible with wrestling, a normal pastime of young men of good family. By the
date of *The Bacchae*, Dionysus was regularly represented as
graceful, almost effeminate; indeed he was already accused of
being womanish in one of Aeschylus' lost plays about him.
The historical and psychological reasons for this conception
are hard to define, and may have been affected by independent
developments in cult and cult-images. That priests sometimes
adopt feminine clothing to increase their effectiveness is probably of small relevance here. More attractive is the suggestion
made by Dodds that the god's effeminacy may be due to the
influence of Asiatic parallels of the consort-god type. In any
event, as a deity whose devotees were predominantly female,
he is likely to be represented as young and desirable; and persistent sexual association with women was held by most Greeks
to make a man less, not more, virile. The poet makes ingenious
use of the tension between the innocent view of Dionysus expressed by the Chorus, the ambiguous picture of the god in the
late fifth century B.C., and the individual sexual prurience of
Pentheus.

PENTHEUS And how is it that you introduce these rites into
Hellas?   465

DIONYSUS Dionysus himself initiated me, the son of Zeus.

PENTHEUS There is some local Zeus there, who begets new
gods?

DIONYSUS No, it was the Zeus who yoked Semele in marriage here.

PENTHEUS Did he constrain you at night, or before your
eyes?

DIONYSUS We were face to face, and he freely grants me
his rituals.   470

PENTHEUS These rituals of yours—what form do they take?

DIONYSUS They may not be uttered to those of men who
are not bacchants.

PENTHEUS And what gain do they bring to those who sacrifice?

DIONYSUS It is not lawful for you to hear—though it is
worth knowing!

PENTHEUS You have counterfeited this answer well, to make
me want to hear!   475

---

466 Not a very explicit reply, but stichomythia, like real conversation, sometimes suppresses stages in an argument.

467 PENTHEUS takes up the incidental description "son of Zeus"
and makes a new sneer out of it: there can be no real Zeus, he
thinks, outside Hellas.

469 The insulting implication is that the stranger's initiation was
illusory, a mere dream.

473 Sacrifice was not an important element in the worship of
DIONYSUS, and PENTHEUS displays his ignorance and misunder-
standing by implying that it was.

475 The first admission of a reluctant curiosity that will grow into
an obsession.

DIONYSUS The god's rites are hostile to the one who prac-
tises impiety.

PENTHEUS Since you claim that you saw the god plainly,
what was his nature?

DIONYSUS Whatever he wished to have; it was not I that
determined this.

PENTHEUS Again you have cleverly diverted the question,
though your words are meaningless.

DIONYSUS He who talks wisdom to an ignorant man will
seem out of his senses.   480

PENTHEUS You came here first, to introduce the god?

DIONYSUS Every foreigner dances in these rites.

PENTHEUS Yes, because they are less sensible than Hellenes.

DIONYSUS In this case, rather, they are fully sensible; but
their customs differ.

PENTHEUS Do you celebrate your sacred acts at night or by
day?   485

DIONYSUS At night for the most part. Darkness possesses
solemnity.

PENTHEUS Darkness brings deceit and corruption against
women!

---

480 wisdom: again the emphasis on *sophon*; cf. notes on 179, 395.

482 Again a slight ellipse: DIONYSUS has come to Hellas because
the work of spreading his cult in Asia is completed; cf. 20–22.

483f PENTHEUS' prejudice that foreigners are necessarily inferior
would be regarded as somewhat old-fashioned by many members of Euripides' audience, who would have been influenced
by the new interest in comparative ethnology and by a fash-
ionable if reluctant admiration for certain Persian institutions.
Euripides had satirized the same prejudice before, especially in
his *Medea*; but it dies hard, and traces of it survive even in
Plato and Aristotle.

DIONYSUS   Even in daytime one could discover disgraceful behaviour.

PENTHEUS   You must pay penalty for your foul sophistries!

DIONYSUS   And you too, for your stupidity and impiety toward the god.   490

PENTHEUS   How brazen is the bacchic fellow, and not untrained in argument!

DIONYSUS   Tell me what I must suffer—what is the dreadful thing you will do to me?

PENTHEUS   First I shall cut off your delicate locks.

DIONYSUS   My long hair is sacred; I am growing it for the god.

PENTHEUS   Next, hand over this thyrsus that you hold.   495

DIONYSUS   Remove it from me yourself; this is Dionysus' thyrsus that I bear!

PENTHEUS   We shall keep you under guard within prison walls.

DIONYSUS   The god himself shall release me—when I will it.

---

489   PENTHEUS is exasperated by the stranger's calm replies, as is shown by the explosion of three initial *d*'s early in the verse (*dikēn se dounai dei*)—only weakly represented in the "pay penalty" of the translation.

494   Dedicating one's hair to a god—vowing not to cut it until certain conditions have been fulfilled, and then offering up the shorn locks—was a familiar practice, especially in the heroic past. In truth, the stranger is growing his hair "for the god" because he *is* the god. Such ironical references to his real identity, misunderstood by PENTHEUS but plain enough to the audience, are frequent in the conversations that follow (as at 498–502) and do not need pointing out on each occasion.

498   The audience will have observed at 443ff. what PENTHEUS ig-

PENTHEUS *Of course, when you call him, standing among your bacchants!*

DIONYSUS *Even now he is close by and sees what I suffer.* 500

PENTHEUS *Well, where is he? He is not visible to my eyes.*

DIONYSUS *Here, with me; but you, because of your impiety, do not behold him.*

PENTHEUS *Seize this fellow—he scorns both me and Thebes.*

DIONYSUS *I tell you not to bind me—I who am sane, you who are not!*

PENTHEUS *And I say bind you—I whose authority counts more than yours!* 505

DIONYSUS *You do not know what your life is, nor what you are doing, nor who you are.*

PENTHEUS *Pentheus, son of Agaue and Echion as father.*

DIONYSUS *You are apt in your name for falling into misfortune!*

PENTHEUS *Off with you—lock him up close to the horses' mangers so that he sees nothing but gloomy darkness.* 510

---

nored, that religious prisoners are hard to keep in Thebes at present. I doubt whether any reference is intended to DIONYSUS' occasional title of *Lysios,* "releaser," as Dodds suggests.

506f PENTHEUS' arrogant reliance on mundane power and his refusal to understand the first thing about Dionysiac religion amount to a total ignorance of his own nature as a man, of the meaning of his actions, and of the real purpose of life. He misunderstands this criticism even more foolishly than what had preceded and gives an automatic and mindless response, his name and family. Is he already coming under the god's spell, made into a mere puppet?

508 On the name of PENTHEUS, see note on 367.

Do your dances there; and these women you have brought with
   you
as collaborators in evil we shall either sell off,
or I shall stop their hands from this drum-beating din
and own them as household slaves at the looms.

   DIONYSUS   I am ready to go; for what must not be, need not   515
be undergone. Yet punishment for these insults
Dionysus shall exact from you, he who you say does not exist;
for in wronging us, it is him that you cast in chains.

STROPHE 1

CHORUS   Achelous' daughter,

511– This direct threat against the CHORUS accounts for some of
514   their growing sense of insecurity and desire for revenge.

515f Deliberately cryptic: it is divinely determined that DIONYSUS
      shall not be imprisoned; therefore he will not have to suffer
      such degradation (and so consents to undergo the preliminaries
      for his own ends).

519– The *Second Stasimon* is simple and direct; it consists of a single
575   strophic pair of stanzas and an epode, and all except the
      last five verses, which are in Aeolic metres, are in the now famil-
      iar Ionic rhythm (note on 64ff.). The strophe reproaches
      Thebes, of all places, for rejecting the bacchants, and surveys
      once again the story of DIONYSUS' birth there; the antistrophe
      attacks the monstrous PENTHEUS and calls on DIONYSUS to pun-
      ish him and protect his own followers; the epode further in-
      vokes the god and names various places where he might be,
      ending with a prediction of his passage through the land of
      Euripides' Macedonian host. The reflectiveness and the passion-
      ate longings of the previous ode are not to be found here.
      The intervening scene with PENTHEUS has sharpened the
      CHORUS' hatred, fear, and sense of isolation. They express their
      loathing of PENTHEUS by contrasting his earth-born ancestry in
      Thebes with DIONYSUS' birth from fire and Zeus, also in Thebes;
      beneath a surface of mythical elaboration there is a clear struc-

67

queen Dirce, fair maiden,   520
you it was who once in your streams
    received the infant of Zeus,
when into his thigh, out of undying fire, Zeus the begetter had snatched
him with this cry: 525
"Go, Dithyrambus, pass into

---

ture of contrast between strophe and antistrophe. The epode invokes the god in conventional terms, and the closing reference to the river Lydias, though flat, sharpens the shock of the god's cry, which follows. As a whole the ode is of exceptional beauty, its language and rhythms fluid and lyrical, its transitions from theme to theme lively yet gentle.

519 The river Achelōus in western Greece was the largest of those within the boundaries of classical Hellas and was evidently thought of as "parent" of all the others. At *Iliad* 21. 195, it is extravagantly linked with the surrounding river Okeanos itself. Dirce is one of the two rivers of Thebes (cf. 5); that the infant was washed in Dirce between his two births is fresh information.

526 Also new is the account of how Dionysus gained the title Dithyrambus. The dithyramb is a genre of choral song sacred to Dionysus; the Chorus assumes that the title came first, but in fact it probably derives from the song. They must have in mind an etymology connected with the double birth, such as that adopted by later grammarians from the superficial resemblance with words for "twice" (*dis*) and "door" (*thura*), i.e., of birth. Such an etymology is in fact fantastic, and not only because of the length of the vowels in *Dī-* and *dīs*; but the audience may be expected to have known of it, especially since every tragic festival included a contest for dithyrambic choirs, and the meaning of the term must have been widely discussed. Perhaps the real association is with *thriambos*, "triumph." It may be asked why, in any event, the Chorus harps on the story of the double birth. The answer is that each time something fresh is added; also these episodes from the life of the god

this male womb of mine;
I reveal you, O Bacchic
one, to Thebes, to call by this name."
But you, O blessed Dirce,   530
thrust me away, when I keep within you
my garland-bearing companies.
Why do you reject me? Why do you flee from
*   me?*
Still—by the grape-clustered
grace of Dionysus' vine!—   535
still shall you show concern for Bromios.   536

ANTISTROPHE 1

He reveals his chthonic   538

---

are essential and traditional elements in a hymn, and many of
the choral passages in this play—the Parodos above all—are
overtly devotional and hymnodic in character. Moreover it is part
of the CHORUS' case that the god's birthplace, if anywhere,
should receive him; so the story of the birth is especially relevant. Nevertheless the pressing of the etymology here seems a
little automatic, a little arid.

528 *I reveal:* a common verb, but one regularly used for the reve-
lation by a god of details of his cult.

530— Dirce stands for Thebes, which does not allow the CHORUS to
532 perform its worship. Line 531, "when I keep within you," is a
little puzzling; but "within" makes sense enough when applied
to the town or region for which the river stands, though not
for the river understood literally.

538— PENTHEUS' father Echion (cf. 507) was one of the original
542 Sown Men, who grew from the dragon's teeth sown by CADMUS.
Thus he was "chthonic," meaning "of the earth"; indeed his
very name signifies something like "snake." But the earth also
breeds monsters, and this helps to explain the unexpectedly
monstrous nature revealed—the verb is the same as in 528—
by PENTHEUS.

race, and his descent from the dragon,
does Pentheus, whom Echion   540
   the chthonic one engendered
as a wild-faced monster, not a human
being, but like a murderous
giant who fights against the gods;
who will fasten me, the servant   545
of Bromios, soon in his toils,
and holds within his house
even now my fellow-dancer,
in dark dungeon hidden away.
Do you behold this, O son of Zeus,   550
Dionysus, your ministers
in the toils of violent compulsion?
Come, shaking your gold-gleaming
thyrsus, Lord, over Olympus,

543f   He is like one of the Giants, who were themselves born from the earth—in full armour, indeed, just like the Sown Men of Thebes. They came to be regarded as monstrous in size and sometimes in shape, and they symbolize violence and anarchy; like the Titans, they fought against the the new Olympian gods led by Zeus, who had to bring in Heracles to defeat them.

548   The Chorus has no conscious inkling of its leader's divine identity.

551   *ministers*: literally "proclaimers," "forthtellers," those who announce the power of the god. English "prophet" is derived from the same word in a later application.

554   *over Olympus*: or "down from Olympus" (Dodds), which entails a slight change in the transmitted text. (The mistaking of Greek *upsilon* for *nu*, which would be the case here, was easy after about A.D. 1100, when the form of the letters was very similar; it was more difficult before. But the error could be aural rather than visual.) Dionysus is mainly thought of in the verses that follow as being somewhere in northern Greece

70

and contain the insolence of a murderous man!   555

EPODE

Where then on Nysa, rearer
  of beasts, do you lead with the thyrsus
your bands, O Dionysus, or
  on the Corycian peaks?

—in Thrace, in Pieria, or on Olympus itself; he would therefore have to traverse the region of Olympus to return to
Thebes. But perhaps "Olympus" and the specific image of the
god with his followers favour the particular mountain rather
than the general region, and also look forward to 560f.

556ff A common, almost universal element of invocations was the
listing of places where the deity might be—usually his favourite
or best known cult-places. In the case of DIONYSUS a slight com-
plication arises, and the distinction between where he might
now be and where he would be likely to be in the future (when
his cult would become firmly established) is not very clearly
drawn.

556 Nysa was a mountain associated with a different story of resistance to DIONYSUS, that by Lycurgus, which formed the basis
of Aeschylus' tetralogy (pp. 2f.). In the one substantial reference to the god in Homer we learn that Lycurgus, son of
Dryas, chased the "nurses" of frenzied DIONYSUS over Nysa,
wielding an ox-goad or an axe (*Iliad* 6. 130ff.). Homer's Lycurgus was probably, and Aeschylus' was certainly, from Thrace,
and that is where Euripides too must envisage Mount Nysa.
The name seems to have been attached to several mountains
where the worship of DIONYSUS was celebrated, and it is conceivable that the name of the god himself is derived from it.
In a (not very early) *Homeric Hymn* (I, 8f.) Mount Nysa is
even said to be close to the streams of Egypt!

559 The "Corycian peaks" refer to Mount Parnassus, where there
was a famous Corycian cave (there was a cave of the same
name in southern Asia Minor, but the Delphic one must surely

71

Or perhaps in the wooded   560
recesses of Olympus, where
once on a time Orpheus, playing his lyre,
drew to him trees by his music,
drew to him untamed beasts?
   O blessed Pieria,   565
Euios honours you, and will come
to dance together with bacchic
      rites, and crossing
the swift-flowing Axios will lead

---

be meant). The peaks are the same as the "twin peaks" of 307. The only difficulty is that Dionysus had not yet established his worship at Delphi at 306–8; but the Chorus seems to feel that although the god came to Thebes first (20), he is even now spreading his worship to other regions, other mountains of Hellas.

562 Orpheus came from Thrace, with which Dionysus had special connections (note on 556), and the two figures—one a god, the other more than an ordinary man—were sometimes associated. Both have exceptional powers over the world of Nature; but in Aeschylus' lost *Bassarids* it seems possible that Orpheus himself resisted Dionysus and suffered the usual consequences for it. Here Orpheus is placed on Olympus, rather, perhaps because of his affiliation with the Muses (note on 410).

565 On Pieria, see note on 410.

566 *Euios:* that is, Dionysus, the god of the ritual cry "euoi" (see note on 141).

569ff The Axios and Lydias were two rivers of Thrace that Dionysus would have to cross if he were moving down from there back to Olympus and Thebes (note on 554). Lydias is especially complimented, probably because it irrigated the land (which was in fact a "land of good horses") of Archelaus, the Macedonian king at whose court Euripides wrote this play. He had used an almost identical description of a quite different river in an earlier play (*Hecuba* 451ff.), and it is not surprising that the

> *his whirling Maenads—*   570
> *crossing, too, father Lydias, the*
> *giver of happiness to mortals*
> *and prosperity; who, I have heard,*
> *with the fairest of waters makes glisten*
> *that land of good horses.*   575

DIONYSUS   *Io*

---

present passage sounds rather formulaic. It is certainly not the strongest possible ending for the ode (but see note on 519–75).

576– *Scene 3, 576–861*: This long, central scene is divided into three
861 parts: (1) the palace miracles, seen first from outside and then, through the stranger's report, from within; (2) the first MESSENGER's speech from Cithaeron—a detailed eye-witness account of remarkable happenings among the maddened bacchants on the mountain; (3) the second long encounter between PENTHEUS and DIONYSUS, in which PENTHEUS is gradually worn down and persuaded to dress as a woman.

The unusual length of the scene is surely deliberate; it forms the central core of the play, and the CHORUS is kept subordinate, an interested spectator and occasional commentator. The main dialogues are separated by a circumstantial account of events on Cithaeron, which is in deliberate contrast to the purer tone of the CHORUS' descriptions of its own worship. When PENTHEUS is finally ready for the slaughter, the CHORUS will sing again in a new, more hysterical key, to mark the beginning of the play's last and most openly disturbing phase.

576– The god's escape from imprisonment amid fire and earthquake
603 seems to have been a traditional theme in the stories of his overcoming resistance to his cult, and it occurred in some form in Aeschylus' lost Lycurgus-play *Edonians*. In Euripides' version of the theme the divine voice of DIONYSUS sounds offstage; the god shows in a terrifying way that he has heard the CHORUS' prayer in the ode just completed for his aid and presence in Thebes. He calls on the spirit of earthquake to shake PENTHEUS' palace, and this actually happens: the architrave of the front

listen to my, listen to my voice,
Io Bacchai, Io Bacchai!

CHORUS   *What is this cry, what is this and from where,*
    of Euios that summoned me?

DIONYSUS   *Io, Io, again I speak,*   580
    the son of Semele, the son of Zeus!

CHORUS   *Io, Io, master, master,*
    come then to our
    company, O Bromios, Bromios!

DIONYSUS   *Heave the earth's floor, you spirit of Earthquake!*   585

---

portico (which must have been represented at the back of the stage) splits asunder (591f.). He then summons fire, and the flames on Semele's tomb (cf. 8) are seen to blaze up (597–99; cf. 623f.). Admittedly the whole palace is not burned down, as DIONYSUS implies it will be at 595, nor is it utterly destroyed by the earthquake as the CHORUS suggests at 602f. Yet these miracles are not just illusions suffered by the CHORUS, as Verrall believed: Greek scenic resources, slight though they were, could have produced an adequate effect. More important, if Euripides had wished to show the CHORUS as suffering from a divinely inspired delusion, he could and would have made this quite clear to the audience. The disguised DIONYSUS reports both fire and earthquake at 622ff.; if they did not take place, then neither did PENTHEUS' hysterical reaction to them, and the whole central scene is fatally weakened.

The metre of this choral dialogue makes a subtle transition from the end of the preceding ode to the trochaic tetrameters of 604ff. (see note on 604–41): it begins with various Aeolic verses and then becomes mainly trochaic (the trochee is – ∪), though with some excited runs of dactyls, as at 594f.

577 "Ῐ̆ο" is an exclamation used in lyric metres, most commonly for the invocation of gods; it is usually repeated, as here.

579 *Euios*: DIONYSUS, from the ritual cry "*euoi*" (note on 141).

585ff *Heave*: a conjectural supplement, evidently necessary. Part of

74

CHORUS	*Ah, ah,*
	quickly will Pentheus' halls be shaken
	apart in collapse!
	Dionysus pervades these halls:
	revere him.—We revere him, O! 590
	—Do you see these stone lintels on the columns
	flying asunder? It is Bromios who
	raises the cry within the building.
DIONYSUS	*Kindle the bright torch of lightning;*
	consume, consume Pentheus' house! 595
CHORUS	*Ah, ah,*
	do you not see fire, do you not behold it
	around Semele's holy tomb, the flame
	(which when lightning-struck she left)
	of Zeus' thunderbolt?
	Cast to the ground, cast your trembling 600
	bodies, Maenads;

---

what follows is divided between different members of the CHORUS or between two semichoruses—so, certainly, is 590; but most could be sung, excitedly indeed, by the whole group. The dashes in 590 and 591 denote the interchange between the two groups.

593 *raises the cry*: the *alalagē* is a ritual shout especially associated with the cult of DIONYSUS and is here represented by the "Io Bacchai, Io Bacchai" of 577.

600– The CHORUS fling themselves to the ground in terror. The
603 whole scene is spectacular beyond the usual limits of Greek tragedy. The urgent voice of the god breaking into the melancholy mood of the end of the stasimon, the sudden excitement of the CHORUS, the earthquake, the recognition that the god is present, the blazing fire, and the mounting hysteria of the women—even a modern producer cannot fail to make something of this, and even a modern audience, bred on sensational effects, cannot fail to be moved.

75

for the Lord will come upon, will overthrow
these halls, the offspring of Zeus.

DIONYSUS   *Alien women, thus utterly struck with terror*
are you fallen to the ground? You felt, it seems, the Bacchic god   605
shaking apart the house of Pentheus. But raise up
your bodies and take courage, rid your flesh of trembling.

CHORUS   *O supreme light of our ecstatic worship*
how gladly I gaze on you, I who had desolate loneliness!

DIONYSUS   *Did you fall into despair when I was escorted*
within,   610
thinking that I should be flung into Pentheus' dark dungeons?

CHORUS   *How could I not? What protector had I, if you*
encountered disaster?
But how were you set free, after your encounter with that
unholy man?

DIONYSUS   *Myself I rescued myself, easily, without effort.*

CHORUS   *But did he not tie your hands in captive knots?*   615

604– DIONYSUS enters in his disguise of the CHORUS' human leader,
641   the Lydian stranger. His subsequent exchange with them and
his account of the strange events offstage are in trochaic tetrameters (verses composed basically of four double-trochee
measures, $- \cup - \cup$), a lilting rhythm that had become almost
obsolete in tragedy. Euripides uses it here partly, no doubt,
because he wished to emphasize the archaic colouring of the
play, and partly because its lightness suited DIONYSUS' relaxed,
almost amused tone.

608   The CHORUS greets their leader as though he were the god
himself, an unintentional recognition of his ambiguity.

612f   The rather unattractive repetition "encountered . . . encounter" reproduces the fortuitous use of the same Greek
verb at the end of each verse (see note on 647), although it is
just possible that the text is corrupt.

76

DIONYSUS *This was just the ignominy I did him, that he*
  thought he was binding me
but neither touched nor laid hands on me, but fed on empty
  hopes.
He found a bull by the stalls where he took me and locked me
  up,
and round his knees and hooves he cast his knots,
panting out his rage, dripping sweat from his body,   620
setting his teeth to his lips. But I close by
was peacefully sitting and watching. It was during this time
that Bacchus came, and shook up the palace, and on his
  mother's tomb
made the fire blaze up; but Pentheus, when he saw it, thinking
  the palace on fire,
rushed one way, then another, bidding his household servants
  bring   625
Achelous' water; and every slave was hard at this work, his labour
  in vain.
But Pentheus left off this toil, since I seemed to have escaped,
and seizing a dark sword he dashes into the palace.

616ff DIONYSUS hardly bothers to hide his supernatural powers. The
  CHORUS at this point will accept almost anything he says as
  true; in any case they were used to strange things happening in
  the worship of their god, and the arrival of their "light" and
  "protector" (608, 612) in the midst of their terror and loneliness seems particularly providential.

617f The Greek has "us" for the "me" (three times) of the translation; only DIONYSUS, of course, is involved. Greek does sometimes use plural for singular in the first person, both in the elevated and in the intimate style.

622 Again the emphasis on DIONYSUS' calmness; so also at 636 and
  640.

625f *Achelous' water*: literally, just "Achelous" (note on 519), an
  artificial figure of speech, which here, perhaps, adds to the absurdity of PENTHEUS' actions.

And then Bromios, as it seems to me—what I say is just my
    opinion—
made a phantom out in the courtyard; and Pentheus, charging
    at it,   630
rushed and pierced the shining air as though it were me he was
    slaughtering.
In addition, the Bacchic god subjects him to these other
    humiliations:
he broke the building to the ground—everything is smashed up,
a bitter outcome of my captivity for him to see; in weariness
he drops his sword and lies exhausted—for against a god,
    though a mere man himself,   635
he had dared to join battle. Peacefully I walked out
of the building, and have come to you, paying no heed to
    Pentheus.
As it seems to me (at least, a footstep sounds inside the halls)
he will be here at the entrance without delay. Whatever will he
    say, after all this?
In any case I shall take him lightly, even if he comes breathing
    arrogance;   640
for it is the quality of a wise man to exercise restrained good
    temper.

    PENTHEUS   I have been outraged! The stranger has escaped
    me,

---

633   Logic and the silence of characters who come on later require
that it be the stable in which DIONYSUS had been imprisoned,
and not the whole palace, that collapses. If so, this verse describes an event later than the first earthquake of 623 and
585ff. Yet the Greek makes no clear distinction, and closely
similar words are used for what is translated as "palace" in 623,
624, and 628, and as "building" in 633.

640f Again the calmness is emphasized, as it was at 622 and 636;
but this time it is stated in entirely human terms—partly to
carry on the didactic argument about the nature of wisdom,
which runs through the play, partly to emphasize the god's
human role.

who just now was under constraint in chains.
Aaah—
this is the man here! What is this? How are you to be seen   645
by the gate, in front of my house? How did you get outside?

DIONYSUS   Stop! and put a quiet stop to your temper.

PENTHEUS   How did you escape your bonds and pass outside?

DIONYSUS   Did I not say—or did you not hear me?—that
someone would release me?

PENTHEUS   Who? These are strange statements you persist in
making.   650

DIONYSUS   He who grows for men the thick-clustered vine.

PENTHEUS   You insulted Dionysus by naming this so-called
benefit!

---

647   The repetition of the word "stop" gives some idea of the not
very elegant Greek: literally, "stay your foot and put a calm
foot to your rage." Admittedly Euripides was often indifferent
to casual recurrences of the same word over a short space; but
here the effect is perhaps intentional, a kind of heartiness or
jocularity that shows that DIONYSUS does not take PENTHEUS
very seriously.

651–   There seems to be a serious interruption in the sequence of
653   thought here, and most critics have supposed that at least one
verse has been lost, either after 651 or (as accepted here) after
652. The implication of 652 is in any event not certain, although
PENTHEUS seems to be referring again (if he is the speaker) to
the deleterious effects of wine on women. PENTHEUS' sudden
command in 653 seems to presuppose a remark by the stranger
more provocative than what we have—for example, something
like "Moreover the god still stands near me, to protect me." In
the passage as a whole DIONYSUS fulfills his traditional role as
the great miracle-worker; so also in the *Homeric Hymn* (VII,
13f., 34ff.), where release from bondage and the growth of the
vine had already been associated.

DIONYSUS . . .

PENTHEUS *I command the whole fortress to be surrounded and closed off!*

DIONYSUS *What then? Do not gods pass even over walls?*

PENTHEUS *You are clever, very clever, except in that in which you should be clever!* 655

DIONYSUS *In what I should most be, in this I am clever through and through.*
But first listen to what this man here has to report
who is newly arrived from the mountain with a message for you;
be assured that we shall stay, we shall not escape.

MESSENGER *Pentheus, commander of this Theban land,* 660
I come from Cithaeron, where never
abate the glistening falls of white snow.

PENTHEUS *What urgent message have you come to deliver?*

MESSENGER *Having seen the sacred bacchants, who flung in frenzy their pale limbs out of this land,* 665
I have come in desire to tell you and the city, lord,
what amazing things they perform, things greater than miracles.
But I want to hear whether with freedom of speech
I am to tell you the news from there, or whether to trim the tale;
for I fear your heart's impetuosity, lord, 670
and your keenness of temper and excess of royal disposition.

PENTHEUS *Speak out, since in any event you shall be unharmed by me;*
for against the righteous one should not be angry.

655f Again the cardinal epithet *sophos*, this time certainly implying "clever" rather than "wise."

661f A poetical exaggeration, whether the meaning is that it never stops snowing on Cithaeron or that snow lies there throughout the year.

673 A piece of hypocrisy, no doubt, coming from PENTHEUS; al-

But the more terrible the things you say about the bacchants
the more this man here, who insinuated his arts   675
into the women, we shall subject to punishment.

MESSENGER   The grazing herds of cattle were just ascending
toward the uplands, at the time when the sun
sends out his rays to warm the earth;
and I see three bands of women dancers,   680
of which Autonoe was leader of one, of the second
your mother Agaue, and Ino of the third.
All were sleeping with bodies relaxed,
some leaning their backs against a fir tree's foliage,
others among oak leaves resting their heads on the ground,   685
carelessly, but decently—it is not as you say,
that drunken from the mixing bowl and to the skirl of the flute
they hunt in the woods for the Cyprian's pleasure, going off one
        by one.
Then your mother gave a ritual shriek, standing up
in the midst of the bacchants, for them to shake their bodies
        out of sleep,   690
when she heard the lowing of the horned cattle.
And they cast off luxuriant sleep from their eyes

---

though the picture of the short-tempered ruler—conveyed by
what the MESSENGER has just said to him—is to a large extent
conventional, and Euripides makes no attempt here to suggest
that PENTHEUS is especially bad in this respect.

677– The cowherd's speech is a brilliant piece of description, in the
774   main both lyrical and explicit, and it needs relatively little de-
      tailed comment.

680   I see: such historic presents are scattered through the narrative
      here, and I translate them literally to reproduce their graphic
      quality.

686   but decently: in paradoxical contrast with "carelessly"; an idea
      repeated in the bacchants' "surprisingly under control" at 940.

689   ritual shriek: see note on 24f.

and leapt to their feet, a miracle of discipline to behold,
women young and old and girls still unmarried.
And first they let down their hair on their shoulders   695
and pulled up their fawnskins—as many as had undone
the knots that held them—and the dappled skins
they girdled with snakes that licked their cheeks.
Some of the women held in their arms a roe
or wild wolf cubs, and gave them white milk—   700
those who had newly given birth, whose breasts were still swollen,
and who had left behind their babies. On their heads they put
     garlands
of ivy and oak and flowering bryony.
Someone grasped a thyrsus and struck it into a rock
from which a dewy stream of water leaps out;   705
another struck her rod on the ground
and for her the god sent up a spring of wine;
and those who had a desire for the white drink

---

693   Again the women's orderliness is stressed, in rebuttal of PEN-
     THEUS' exotic fancies. And yet Euripides could have made
     these false maenads licentious—after all they commit other
     atypical excesses. He chose not to, perhaps to avoid playing on
     a popular prejudice and so weakening the CHORUS' emphasis on
     the benign aspects of its cult.

695   Presumably they had put up their hair to sleep, but they now let
     it down to emphasize their wildness and abandon.

698   Do these snakes lick their own cheeks, in a loose reference to
     the appearance of their flicking tongues, or do they rear up and
     lick the women's? The latter interpretation seems strained but
     may be right in view of 767f., a fuller passage which seems
     reminiscent of this one and in which the snakes definitely lick
     the maenads' cheeks.

708   the white drink: a literal translation. The cowherd's language,
     as in other messenger-speeches in tragedy, can be stilted and
     pretentious at times; occasional genre touches break the flow
     of a description that the poet otherwise makes as cruel and
     beautiful as he can. From about 695 to 711 the cowherd's won-

scraped the ground with their fingertips
and had jets of milk; and from out of the ivied   710
thyrsi, sweet streams of honey dripped.
So that, had you been there, the god you now condemn
you would have courted with prayers because of these sights.
   We cowherds and shepherds gathered together
to vie with each other in sharing our own account   715
of what strange and marvellous things they were doing.
And one who frequented the town and was glib with words
addressed us all: "O you who on the holy plateaus
of the mountains dwell, is it your wish that we hunt
Pentheus' mother Agaue away from the bacchic dances   720
and so oblige our lord?" His suggestion seemed to us
a good one, and we lie in ambush hiding ourselves
in the bushes' foliage. The women, at the appointed
hour, began to move the thyrsus into bacchic dances,
calling in unison on Bromios as Iacchus,   725
the offspring of Zeus; and all the mountain and its wild creatures

---

der at what he saw is reflected in an elevated, even portentous
style.

725 *Iacchus:* another of DIONYSUS' cult-titles, probably connected
with the verb *iachein*, "to give a ritual cry," and developed particularly in Eleusis, where DIONYSUS became associated with the
famous mysteries of Demeter.

726f This marvellous sentence was thought bold in antiquity; it is
probably a development of a verse from one of Aeschylus' Lycurgus plays, "the hall is possessed by the god, the building
[*bakcheuei*], performs bacchic worship," and is not far removed
from expressions like "the earth all around laughed" in Homer
(*Iliad* 19. 362). In fact the Euripidean sentence is less bold
than these in its metaphorical quality: the whole mountain
joins in the dances since all its wild creatures rush around, and
the trees and undergrowth move to the wind of the maenads'
running.

joined in bacchic worship, and nothing remained unmoved by
    their running.
   Agaue chances to jump close by me
and I leaped out, wanting to seize her,
deserting the ambush place where I was hiding myself.   730
She shouted out, "O my coursing hounds,
we are hunted by these men; but follow me,
follow, armed with your thyrsi in your hands!"
So we took to our heels and escaped
being torn to pieces by the bacchants; but they attacked the
    grazing   735
heifers, with hand that bore no steel.
And one you could have seen holding asunder in her hands
a tight-uddered, young, bellowing heifer;
while others were tearing full-grown cows to pieces.
You could have seen ribs, or a cloven hoof,   740
being hurled to and fro; and these hung
dripping under the fir trees, all mixed with blood.
Bulls that were arrogant before, with rage
in their horns, stumbled to the ground,
borne down by the countless hands of girls.   745
The garments of flesh were drawn apart more quickly
than you could close the lids over your royal eyes.

734– The MESSENGER and his friends had no doubt that the bacchants
736   were really dangerous—as the women then demonstrated by
turning their wrath on the cattle. A *sparagmos*, a tearing-to-
pieces, actually takes place. It is a caricature, in a way, of the
"normal" climax of bacchic frenzy as described by the true
bacchants of the CHORUS at 138f.; and yet it gives a sinister
foretaste of what is to happen to the next intruder to wait in
secret on the mountain.

743   *with rage in their horns:* literally, "being enraged into [or as far
as] the horn," the probable meaning being that their rage made
them lower their horns for the charge.

747   Again the pretentious phraseology, whose effect at this point is
to provide a brief moment of almost comic relief.

The women move like birds lifted by their flight
over the plains stretched out below, which by the streams of
    Asopus
send forth the Thebans' fertile corn crop;   750
and on Hysiae and Erythrae, which lie on the lower slopes
of Cithaeron, like enemies
they fell, and turned everything
upside down. They snatched children from their homes;
and whatever they set on their shoulders stuck there   755
without being tied, and did not fall to the dark ground—
not bronze, not iron; and upon their locks
they carried fire and it did not burn them. The villagers, in rage
at being plundered by the bacchants, rushed to arms.
The sight that followed was strange to see, lord;   760
for the men's pointed spears drew no blood,
but the women, discharging thyrsi from their hands,
wounded the men and made them turn their backs in flight:
women did this to men—some god must have helped them!
Back they went to the place they had started from,   765

---

749   The river Asopus ran between Thebes and the foot of Cithae-
      ron; cf. 1044.

751   Hysiae and Erythrae were villages, also mentioned by Herod-
      otus in relation to the Persian War.

757   The specification of the metals (which presumably refer to
      cooking pots and other utensils plundered from the houses—it
      has been suggested that bronze refers to pots, iron to agricul-
      tural implements) has caused some critical surprise, and admit-
      tedly the children of 754 are dismissed rather quickly. But if
      heavy and rounded objects will stick, others will do so too; there
      is little need to suppose a gap in the text. Dodds observes that
      unusual powers of balance, as well as the ability to endure pain
      by fire, are attested for ecstatic cults in other parts of the
      world.

765– Strictly, the MESSENGER would be unlikely to know this (would
768   he and his friends continue to spy on the women after their
      narrow escape at 734f.?); but the convention of the messenger-
      speech allowed this kind of departure from realism.

to the very springs the god sent up for them;
they washed off the blood, while the drops from their cheeks
the snakes cleansed from the skin with their tongues.
  So this god, master, whoever he is,
receive him into this land, since he is great in other things, too,   770
but especially, I hear, they say that he
has given to men the vine that ends pain.
If wine were no more, then Cypris is no more
nor anything else delightful for mankind.

  CHORUS   I am afraid of speaking my words out freely   775
to the supreme ruler, but nevertheless it shall be said:
Dionysus is the equal of any of the gods!

  PENTHEUS   Already close by it blazes up like fire,

767f It is remarkable how the poet manages to avoid any strong
      effect of absurdity in describing these wonders. The naiveté of
      the MESSENGER palliates any uneasiness we may have.

769– The concluding moral, drawn after the fashion of tragic mes-
774   sengers, is supported by reasons the simplicity of which reflects
      the cowherd's own character: it is DIONYSUS' gift of wine, and
      therefore of love and pleasure, that is emphasized here and not
      the deeper joys of his worship as the CHORUS understands them.
      Cypris in 773 is of course Aphrodite; cf. 402f. and note on 315.

778– In this last section of the great central scene PENTHEUS pays no
861   attention to the miracles he has heard described, just as he had
      ignored the implications of his encounter with the Bacchic
      stranger in the stables. He concentrates on the mere unruliness
      of the maenads on Cithaeron, and is especially enraged by their
      being women (785f.); in his plan to shed their blood he seems
      to forget that some of them are his own family. At least his
      attention has been diverted from the unmanageable stranger;
      he soon loses his temper with him again, but his obsession with
      the women enables DIONYSUS to tighten his grip on PENTHEUS'
      imagination.

this mad insolence of the bacchants, a huge reproach to the men
    of Hellas!
There must be no hesitation: you, be off to the Electran   780
gate; order all the heavy infantrymen
and the riders of swift-footed horses to parade,
and all who ply light shields and make the bowstring
sing with their hand, since we shall march against
the bacchants. No, this exceeds all bounds,   785
if at the hands of women we are to suffer what we do!
    Exit MESSENGER.

  DIONYSUS   You obey not at all, although you hear my words,
Pentheus. Though I am badly treated by you, yet
I tell you: do not raise arms against a god;
keep your peace; Bromios will not tolerate   790
your moving the bacchants from the mountains that ring with
    the sacred cry!

  PENTHEUS   Stop preaching at me! You have escaped from
    prison,
so hold onto your freedom! Or shall I turn back the course of
punishment upon you?

---

779   *a huge reproach to the men of Hellas*: both for the unrestrained
     nature of the cult and for the civil disorders it engenders.

780f The gate of Electra faced southward, toward Cithaeron.

781– The decorative and artificial language reminds one of PENTHEUS
784   calling water "Achelous" at 625f., another situation that called
     for action rather than for high-flown language. Here, perhaps,
     it helps to make him look absurd, although Homer's *Iliad* had
     set a precedent for martial description in an artificial style.

788– Is DIONYSUS serious in this advice, whose conciliatory tone is
790   continued in the offer of 802 and 804? His prediction in the
     Prologue did not exclude the idea; but probably Euripides just
     wants to make PENTHEUS' obstinate folly even plainer.

793   *shall I turn back the course of punishment . . . ?*: the stranger
     has nearly been punished but has been spared; punishment has,
     as it were, gone past him, but its path can be reversed.

DIONYSUS *I would sacrifice to him, rather than in rage*
kick *against the pricks, a mortal against a god!*   795

PENTHEUS *I shall sacrifice all right, stirring up—as they
    deserve—*
plenty *of female bloodshed in the glades of Cithaeron!*

DIONYSUS *You will be put to flight, all of you; what a dis-
    grace to turn*
your *shields of wrought bronze before the thyrsi of the bac-
    chants!*

PENTHEUS *Quite unmanageable is this stranger we are en-
    tangled with,*   800
who *will not hold his tongue, whatever is done to him.*

DIONYSUS *Sir, it is still possible to arrange this satisfactorily.*

PENTHEUS *By doing what? taking orders from my own slaves?*

DIONYSUS *I shall bring the women here without using
    weapons.*

PENTHEUS *Ah me—now this is the trick you are devising
    against me!*   805

DIONYSUS *What kind of trick, if I wish to save you by my
    arts?*

PENTHEUS *You and the women arranged this between you,
    so as to keep on with your bacchic rites.*

DIONYSUS *Arranged it, yes; so much is true—but with the
    god.*

---

801 *whatever is done to him:* literally, "whether he is being acted
    against or acting"—a favourite Greek idiom, in which universal-
    ity is implied by expressing the polar extremes. Here the mean-
    ing is "in all circumstances."

807 *between you:* i.e., with the maenads on Cithaeron.

PENTHEUS   Bring out my armour; and you, stop talking!

DIONYSUS (confidentially)   Here!   810
Would you like to see them sitting close together, up in the
    hills?

PENTHEUS   Very much indeed—I would give an untold
    weight of gold to do so!

DIONYSUS   What, have you fallen into so great a passion for
    this?

PENTHEUS   I should be pained to see them the worse for
    drink . . .

DIONYSUS   Nevertheless you would enjoy seeing what causes
    you distress?   815

PENTHEUS   Yes, you are right; but in silence, lying low under
    the firs.

810– The god has made his last offer and now turns to compassing
816   PENTHEUS' destruction. PENTHEUS has lost patience again, but
      his attention is suddenly held by the new and dramatic appeal
      to his curiosity.

811   *sitting close together:* literally just "sitting together." There is
      no special suggestion in the Greek verb of any impropriety, but
      one cannot help wondering, especially in view of the exceptional
      enthusiasm of PENTHEUS' response, whether that is not implied.
      His suspicions of licence with men have been refuted by the
      MESSENGER (686–88).

813   PENTHEUS' reply has indicated an almost erotic passion, *eros,*
      to see the women.

814– PENTHEUS temporarily regains the detachment becoming to a
816   ruler; perhaps the term *eros* has given him caution; and yet he
      cannot resist DIONYSUS' next suggestion, that he would enjoy
      seeing even if he professes to disapprove. Indeed he considers
      the matter in a practical light and understands that he must
      watch secretly.

DIONYSUS But they will track you down, even if you come secretly.

PENTHEUS Then I shall come openly—that is a good point.

DIONYSUS Are we to lead you, then, and will you undertake the journey?

PENTHEUS Lead on with all speed; I grudge you any delay. 820

DIONYSUS Then clothe your limbs with linen robes.

PENTHEUS What is this, then? Am I to stop being a man and join the ranks of women?

DIONYSUS Yes, for fear they kill you if you are sighted there as a man.

PENTHEUS Another good reply! How clever you are, and have been all along!

DIONYSUS It is Dionysus who gave us these accomplishments. 825

PENTHEUS How, then, shall we put your good advice into practice?

DIONYSUS I shall go inside the palace with you and dress you myself.

PENTHEUS In what dress? Really a female one? But I am ashamed!

817– The purpose of this exchange is to persuade PENTHEUS not
821   merely to go to Cithaeron, and to go in secret, but also to go
      dressed as a female bacchant. The god's apparent divergence
      from this purpose at 819 also has its point: he takes the oppor-
      tunity of obtaining a formal admission from PENTHEUS that he
      will accept DIONYSUS as guide.

824   *clever*: *sophos* again, with the senses "clever" and "truly wise"
      ambiguously merged.

828– PENTHEUS' shame at the idea of accepting female disguise ap-
836   pears to be diminished as each article of equipment is men-

DIONYSUS You are no longer keen to watch the maenads?

PENTHEUS What kind of costume do you propose to dress
me in?   830

DIONYSUS First, from your head I shall hang down long
tresses.

PENTHEUS And the next feature of my adornment?

DIONYSUS Skirts down to the feet; and on your head will be
a snood.

PENTHEUS And will you equip me with anything else beyond
all this?

DIONYSUS Yes, a thyrsus in your hand and a dappled fawnskin.   835

PENTHEUS No: I could not put on female garb!

DIONYSUS But you will spill blood if you join battle with the
bacchants.

PENTHEUS You are right: I must first go and spy out the
land.

DIONYSUS That would be wiser, at all events, than hunting
down evil with evil.

PENTHEUS And how shall I avoid being seen by the Cadmeians as I pass through the town?   840

---

tioned; he seems fascinated by them—perhaps because they
will make him a bacchant as much as because they will make
him a woman. At 836 he suddenly resists once more, but
temporarily.

837f At 796f. PENTHEUS seemed to be enjoying the idea of spilling
some female blood; now he is deterred by it. Nothing between
accounts for his change of mind, which betokens inconstancy
rather than moral improvement.

DIONYSUS *We shall go by deserted streets, and I shall lead the way.*

PENTHEUS *Anything is preferable to the bacchants mocking at me.*
When we have gone indoors . . . I shall decide on what seems best.

DIONYSUS *As you wish; however you decide, I am ready to comply.*

PENTHEUS *I propose to go within; for either I shall proceed under arms*   845
or I shall obey your counsels.

DIONYSUS *Women, the man is moving into the net*   848
and will come to the bacchants, where he will pay the penalty with his death!   847
Dionysus, now the action is yours—for you are not far off.
Let us take vengeance on him; first put him out of his mind,   850
loosing upon him the fantasies of madness; for in his senses
he will absolutely refuse to put on women's dress,
but, if he is driving off the road of sanity, he will put it on.

---

842 There is nothing morbid or exceptional in PENTHEUS' desire not to be laughed at by women. This, at least, was a natural feeling for any Greek, let alone a Greek monarch, and it is why the inhibition cannot be easily overcome.

843– This is PENTHEUS' last show of resistance, of still having a mind
846 of his own. In fact, as DIONYSUS reveals at 848, he is already caught.

845 *within:* not in the Greek. PENTHEUS probably means that he will enter the palace rather than that he will go to Cithaeron (which is in any event assumed).

850 Formally this implies that PENTHEUS has not been out of his mind before. Yet what is meant is probably that a final, extra infatuation is needed to overcome what is evidently a severe blockage: for all his curiosity PENTHEUS finds the indignity of the disguise a deterrent.

I long for him to incur derision from the Thebans
by being led through town disguised as a woman 855
after the earlier threats he tried to terrorize us with!
Now I shall go, to fit the finery he will wear

---

854 It is the god himself, not the human *persona*, who desires open
humiliation and revenge; see 47f., 1377f.

857– Great stress has been laid by the stranger on PENTHEUS' assump-
860 tion of feminine disguise. PENTHEUS has resisted the idea
fiercely, as the god recognizes at 852, and special measures are
needed to make him give way on this point—not even the subtlety of DIONYSUS' arguments could achieve it. Why this emphasis on transvestism? Is it (1) associated with the custom in
certain primitive societies, a custom of which relics might be
seen in one or two Greek cults, of a priest dressing as a woman
to increase his effectiveness in some way? Or is it (2) connected
with wearing the clothes of the other sex in *rites de passage?*
Does it (3) dedicate PENTHEUS to the very god he has resisted,
by dressing him as a worshipper? Is it simply (4) a device to
complete his manifest humiliation? Or is it (5) a perverse man-
ifestation of PENTHEUS' own sexuality, of his jealousy in this
respect of the bacchants? I doubt whether (1) and (2), at least,
have much relevance, though (2) is more attractive than (1),
since PENTHEUS is not a priest but *is* about to pass from life to
death, when such *rites* were relevant. Suggestion (3) is momen-
tarily more persuasive, but for this purpose by itself PENTHEUS
could have been dressed simply as a male bacchant, like CADMUS
and TIRESIAS. Suggestion (4) is certainly relevant, as DIONYSUS'
words at 854–56 show; but it is scarcely adequate by itself, and
it is surely to be reinforced by (5). It is worth remembering,
too, that the traditional story of PENTHEUS' death probably included this motif of his disguise as a maenad. Yet this would be
a variant of an old and widespread theme of death by mistaken
identity—or of the associated theme of the devotee who is
killed by the instruments of his devotion, as Actaeon was killed
by his own hunting dogs for an affront to the goddess of hunting (note on 337–40). In our play these themes are significantly

93

for his journey to Hades, slain by his mother's hands,
on Pentheus; and he shall recognize the son of Zeus,
Dionysus, as a god in perfect essence: 860
most terrible to men, but also most gentle.
    Exit DIONYSUS.

STROPHE 1

CHORUS   *Shall I in night-long dances*

---

    elaborated and are given a psychological colouring that forms an essential part of the whole dramatic structure.

861 The meaning is that DIONYSUS can be both terrible and gentle, according to how one treats him; but the phrasing emphasizes his gentle aspect, ironically for PENTHEUS.

862– The *Third Stasimon* is a song of extraordinary power and beauty,
911 and of more complexity than meets the eye. The CHORUS are heartened by their leader's assurance that PENTHEUS is falling into DIONYSUS' power. Their sense of growing relief causes them to reflect on the sureness of divine vengeance, and their knowledge of this provides adequate happiness for them, at least for the moment. The rhythm of the single strophic pair of stanzas, with a repeated refrain and an epode, is Aeolic in character (note on 64ff.), with the so-called glyconic (– – – ∪ ∪ – ∪ –) as the predominant measure. At the ode's beginning the Lydian bacchants dare to hope that they will some time be free to continue their "nightlong dances," and they think of a fawn who has escaped the hunters and races joyfully by the woods and river. The refrain is in sharp contrast: sententious and cryptic, it concludes that revenge is sweet and is sanctioned by the gods. The antistrophe develops this moralizing trend; in the language of philosophy as much as of pure poetry, it calmly sets out the inescapable power of the gods and the inviolability of established law. The refrain, at its second appearance, has acquired deeper meaning; and the epode achieves an ingenious mediation between the ideas of escape and relief on the one hand and joy in vengeance on the other. One of the

ever set white
foot in bacchic celebration, hurling
my throat to the dewy air of heaven,   865
like a fawn playing in the green
pleasures of a meadow,
when it has escaped the terrifying
   hunt, beyond the watchers,
over the well-woven nets;   870
and, shouting, the huntsman
tautens the hounds to their fastest speed?
With straining and with gales of swift   873
running it bounds over the plain   873
by the river, rejoicing

---

densest of Euripides' odes, it ends with a clear echo of the mood
of the First Stasimon (cf. especially 421–32).

864f *hurling my throat*: the head (for which Greek sometimes uses
"throat" or "neck" in any case, cf. 241) is flung back in a typical bacchic gesture (cf. 930f.), often represented in vase
paintings, which lifts and exposes the throat.

866– The image of the joyous fawn has an obvious resemblance to
876 a developed Homeric simile; yet the care expended on the
huntsman has here (as it might not in a Homeric comparison)
a special relevance to the actual situation—it stresses the theme
of the hunter, which is central to the drama (pp. 13f.). Fawns
symbolize freedom and playfulness in earlier lyric poetry and
elsewhere in Euripides' own work. Here, in a common type of
ring composition, the fawn's joy is described, then the circumstances leading to it are explained, and then the joy itself is
further developed, with a final allusion (875, "solitude") to the
cardinal idea of escape.

866f *green pleasures of a meadow*: an even more striking and unusual phrase in Greek than it seems in English.

872 *tautens the hounds*: literally, "tautens the running of the
hounds."

873 *with . . . running*: literally, "with swift-running gales."

95

in solitude from men and in the shady-   875
leaved forest's saplings.

What is wisdom? Or what fairer

875f   In his note on the passage Dodds has acutely expressed the emphasis in *The Bacchae* on the beauty of Nature viewed quite apart from man; it comes out, too, in some of the descriptions of Mount Cithaeron, notably 1084f. It is a rare attitude for Greek poetry; but is it, as Dodds suggests, quite a "romantic vision"? In one way, yes: Nature is seen as having a life of its own, a force and freedom unaffected by men. In certain Homeric similes drawn from the natural world a human observer is deliberately inserted as a point of reference (e.g., *Iliad* 4. 452ff.); but here, by contrast, the huntsman is described in vivid detail, not only to make the dangers more real, but also to sharpen the antithesis between the ambivalent world of men and the simple solitude of forest and river. Yet the main purpose is Dionysiac or religious rather than romantic: Nature possesses power and freedom as in the remote haunts of Aphrodite and the Graces in the First Stasimon, where "for bacchants it is lawful to hold their rites" (415f.).

877–   The exact meaning of this refrain has been much debated. Its
881   concluding words are certainly a proverb (Plato, *Lysis* 216 C), whose implication seems to have been that one finds "fair" or attractive, and so pursues, what is to one's own advantage. The opening question, too, about the nature of *sophon* (wisdom or cleverness?), is an old one. Now if there is no "fairer gift from the gods in men's eyes" than subduing one's enemies, and since "what is fair is always followed" (literally, "is always dear"), then men are right to pursue their enemies. It will be definition enough of the question about wisdom, at least for the time being, as far as the CHORUS, in its particular situation, is concerned. In fact "fairer" and "fair" are given different values; the former implies "fine," the latter "advantageous," and the CHORUS has no hesitation about accepting the former if it is

gift from the gods in men's eyes
than to hold the hand of power
over the head of one's enemies?   880
   And "what is fair is always followed."

ANTISTROPHE 1

It is slow to stir, but nonetheless
it never fails, the strength

---

definitely allied, as it is by the ambiguity of the Greek word *kalon*, with the latter.

The CHORUS' usual answer to the "what is wisdom?" sort of question, well exemplified in the First Stasimon at 386–401, is different: wisdom consists in obeying the gods and the laws and not aiming too high. This, too, is to be the MESSENGER's conclusion at 1150–52, where "finest" and "wisest" are held to converge in the practice of moderation and veneration of the gods. In the present circumstances, however, the CHORUS finds a special and somewhat sophistic argument for limiting its overriding question to the immediate situation with PENTHEUS. Its attitude might be paraphrased as follows: "What is wisdom? —that is the question we are always asking as one dilemma succeeds another. At present, why look further than following our immediate advantage? To subdue one's enemies is an obvious example of this and has been sanctioned by the gods themselves; therefore wisdom, for us, at this moment, consists in demanding the punishment of PENTHEUS."

882–
890 The power of the gods to act from afar and without effort was a traditional religious belief; as, for example, in Aeschylus, *Suppliant Women* 96–100: "Zeus hurls mortals in destruction from their high-towered expectations, but puts forth no force; everything of the gods is without toil." Traditional, too, was the inevitability of their retribution, as in *Iliad* 4. 160f.: "for even if the Olympian does not at once bring [the oath] to accomplishment, yet he will do so, though late, and to the full . . ."; and the divine stealth, as in Aeschylus, *Persians* 107f.: "What mortal man will avoid the cunning deceit of god?"

of gods; and it brings to correction those
of men who honour senseless folly   885
and fail to foster things divine
in the madness of their judgment.
The gods keep hidden in subtle ways
   the long foot of time, and
hunt down the impious one; for never   890
must a man conceive and practise
what is "better" than the laws.
For it is light expense to believe   893
that this possesses power,   893
whatever it is that constitutes divinity;
and that what is held lawful over length of
                    time   895

---

889   Time itself is envisaged as a runner who surreptitiously and however long the pursuit overtakes his (or rather the gods') victim.

890–   The impiety is committed out of senseless folly (cf. 885–87),
896   and consists in exceeding in thought and deed what is hallowed by immemorial law or custom and established in Nature itself. Going against natural law—which according to the CHORUS means that all gods should be respected, because the divine is supreme—is just what PENTHEUS has done.

895f   Not everything that is "held lawful" "exists by Nature"— indeed the distinction between law or custom and Nature had been made very familiar by the sophists and was widely accepted at the time of *The Bacchae*. In implying that there is no opposition between the two concepts the CHORUS is not being paradoxical; rather it is dealing with one special form of law, for that which is lawful "over length of time" is natural law, not just human custom or man-made law. It was widely accepted that there were certain unwritten laws—like respecting the dead—which were not conventional but rooted in the nature of things; we are reminded of "the traditions of our fathers, from time immemorial our possession," of 201f., strange though those words were in the mouth of TIRESIAS. Here, natural law *exists forever and by Nature.*

What is wisdom? or what fairer
gift from the gods in men's eyes
than to hold the hand of power
over the head of one's enemies? 900
And "what is fair is always followed."

EPODE

Happy the man who from the sea
  escapes the storm and finds harbour;
happy he who has surmounted
  toils; and in different ways one surpasses
                                    another 905
in prosperity and power.
  Besides this, for countless men there are
                                    countless 906

---

is held to include reverence for the gods. Of course this is not quite so decisive in PENTHEUS' case as it is made to appear; PENTHEUS nowhere professes atheism—he just does not see that this new god *is* a god.

902–911 The epode begins with what looks like a renewed expression of joy at the prospect of safety; but more than that is involved (as Dodds has shown after E. Fraenkel), since 902f. and 904f. are also items in a list of different types of happiness, none of which seems to provide a constant and unfailing rule of life:

(1) escaping dangers (902f.)
(2) surmounting toils (904f.)
(3) being successful in various ways (905f.)
(4) being hopeful for the future (907–9).

Of these (1) and (2) are purely retrospective and transient, (3) is uncertain of continuance, and (4) is notoriously fallible. Therefore happiness on a day-to-day basis is all one can reasonably hope for and aim at (910f.), and this accords entirely with the CHORUS' professions of the First Stasimon, especially 397–401 and 430–32.

hopes—some of them 907
reach to the end in prosperity
for mortals, and others depart;
but him whose life day by day 910
is happy do I count blessed.

DIONYSUS You there, who are so eager to see what you
   should not see,
and strive to achieve what should not be sought, Pentheus I
   mean,
come out in front of the palace, let me see you,
wearing the trappings of a woman, a maenad, a bacchant, 915
to spy on your mother and her company.
But you look just like one of Cadmus' daughters!

PENTHEUS Look—I seem to myself to see two suns
and a double Thebes, a double seven-mouthed fortress;
and you appear to lead on ahead of me as a bull, 920

912– *Scene 4,* 912–76: DIONYSUS and then PENTHEUS emerge from
976 the palace. PENTHEUS is now dressed as a female bacchant and
   is completely under the god's power. In his hallucinations lies
   an ambiguous element of sinister truth—he sees the stranger as
   a bull and foresees his mother bringing him back from Cithaeron in her arms. In a conversation in couplets DIONYSUS
   ostensibly humours him; he is no longer making a show of refuta-
   tion or persuasion, as in the previous scenes with PENTHEUS,
   but rather is completely humiliating him and putting the finish-
   ing touches to the degradation of a selfish and unimaginative
   character. PENTHEUS displays in turn an effeminate vanity in his
   new clothes, a sense of physical power that is mad even for a
   bacchant, his old sexual prurience and voyeurism, and a crazy
   boastfulness. The scene ends with the god leading his victim
   offstage toward the mountain and calling on the absent AGAUE
   to prepare his reception there.

920f PENTHEUS has already (618f.) tied up a bull in mistake for
   DIONYSUS; now the stranger seems to him once again to take on
   the form of a bull. (I doubt if 923 implies, as Dodds suggests,

100

and on your head horns seem to grow!
Were you a beast before? For you are certainly a bull now!

DIONYSUS   The god accompanies me—he was not favourable
  before—
and is our ally. Now you see what you should see.

PENTHEUS   What do I look like, then? Do I not seem to have
  Ino's way of standing,   925
or that of Agaue, my mother?

DIONYSUS   I seem to be looking at them in person, when I
  look at you.
But this curl has fallen out of its proper place,
not as I fixed it under the snood.

PENTHEUS   When I was inside I shook my head forward and
  tossed it back   930
and played the bacchant, and so dislodged the curl from its
  place.

DIONYSUS   Well, we whose care it is to look after you
shall put it back in position; now hold your head straight.

---

that PENTHEUS sees a bull-god *in addition to* the stranger, in
spite of his double image of Thebes.) A bull is one of DIONY-
SUS' standard animal manifestations, and the CHORUS will call
on him at 1018f. to "appear as a bull or a many-headed snake
or a fire-blazing lion to behold." We have already learned from
the cowherd that the maenads on Cithaeron have been tearing
bulls to pieces; the connection of the species with the god was
not particularly significant at that point, but now we can see
that the shape of the god and his victim is sometimes the
same; PENTHEUS will be torn to pieces like the cattle, and AGAUE
will suffer the delusion that his head is a lion's (1174), another
of the god's manifestations.

932f DIONYSUS seems to derive special pleasure from pretending to
  serve PENTHEUS while he is actually driving him to his death. In
  part this is in return for the indignities that PENTHEUS had tried

PENTHEUS   *There, you arrange it; for on you we now depend.*

DIONYSUS   *And your girdle is loose, and your dress's pleats*   935
are ruffled where they hang below the ankles.

PENTHEUS   *Yes, I think so too, at least by the right foot—*
but on this side the dress falls correctly by the heel.

DIONYSUS   *You will surely regard me as first among your*
friends
when you see the bacchants surprisingly under control!   940

PENTHEUS   *Shall I look more like a bacchant*
if I hold the thyrsus in the right hand, or in this one?

DIONYSUS   *You must take it in the right hand, and lift it*
in time with the right foot. I congratulate you on your change
of mentality!

PENTHEUS   *Could I carry the glens of Cithaeron,*   945

---

to heap upon him; but I wonder whether the formal corre-
spondence between these verses and 493–96, where PENTHEUS
had wanted to cut the stranger's hair and take away his thyrsus,
is close enough to justify interpreting this as a deliberate reversal, as do Dodds and others.

934   There is a possible double meaning in the Greek that does not
come out in the translation: the words "on you we now depend" can also mean "to you we are now dedicated" (as a
religious offering).

940   It is difficult to think of a harmless meaning for this verse, one
which PENTHEUS might be expected to place on it. Perhaps he is
supposed to pay no attention to it or to be too befuddled to
understand. So also with the last words of 960, unless they are
an aside.

943f   It is not at all sure that the lifting of the right arm and foot
together seemed absurd to Greeks.

945–   The worshippers of DIONYSUS felt full of power and energy; the
954   effects with CADMUS and TIRESIAS were a little pathetic (187–

bacchants and all, on my shoulders?

DIONYSUS   You could if you wished. No, your previous state
   of mind
was not normal, but now you have the one you need.

PENTHEUS   Should we bring levers? Or shall I tear them up
   by hand,
putting a shoulder or arm beneath the peaks?   950

DIONYSUS   Now do not go smashing up the shrines of the
   Nymphs
and Pan's haunts, where he plays his pipes!

PENTHEUS   You are right; victory must not be won by
   physical force
over women. I shall hide my person among the firs.

DIONYSUS   You will be hidden with the hiding that is appropriate   955
for one who comes as a furtive spy on maenads.

PENTHEUS   Yes, and I imagine them as in the thickets, like
   birds,
gripped in the sweetest toils of love-making!

DIONYSUS   Well, you are despatched as a guardian against
   this very thing;
perhaps you will catch them—if you are not caught first.   960

PENTHEUS   Convey me through the middle of the Theban
   land—

---

90); here they are ludicrous. This is madness, not inspiration.
PENTHEUS only calms down when DIONYSUS humours him with
childish talk about Pan and the Nymphs; and then his response
at 953f. is a *non sequitur*—he is incapable of pursuing a single
train of thought for long.

957f The preoccupation with sexual fantasies comes out plainly
here; yet this is only one of PENTHEUS' weaknesses, and by 962
he returns to boastfulness and arrogance.

103

for I am the only man of them to dare this deed!

DIONYSUS   You alone take on the burden for this city, you
    alone;
therefore the necessary contests await you.
Follow, and I shall go as your escort and protector,   965
though another shall bring you back . . .

PENTHEUS   Yes, my mother!

DIONYSUS   . . . as a sight for all.

PENTHEUS   It is for this that I come.

DIONYSUS   You will be carried here . . .

PENTHEUS   That is pampering me . . .

DIONYSUS   . . . in your mother's arms.

PENTHEUS   . . . and you will
    make me really spoiled!

DIONYSUS   Yes, spoiled—in a special way.

PENTHEUS   Well, I am
    touching my deserts.   970

DIONYSUS   Wonderful you are, wonderful, and wonderful the
    experiences you go to meet,

---

964   The "necessary contests," like the "great contest" of 975, will
    be PENTHEUS' fatal encounter with the maenads; but he pre-
    sumably takes the words as a continuation of the idea of "tak-
    ing on the burden for this city," in the preceding verse.

966ff PENTHEUS becomes even more excited at the thought of his
    triumphant return from the expedition, and this is shown by
    his interruptions and by the division of the verses.

971   The Greek word translated as "wonderful" here is deinos,
    which also means "clever," "remarkable," "formidable," "ter-
    rible." Its third use in this verse strongly implies the last mean-
    ing, but PENTHEUS is too infatuated to notice.

so that you will find renown that reaches to the sky.

(He turns in the direction of Cithaeron.)

Stretch out your arms, Agaue, and you her sisters,
daughters of Cadmus; I am leading the youth
to his great contest—and the winner shall be I   975
and Bromios! The rest, the event itself will show.

STROPHE 1

CHORUS   Go forth, swift hounds of Frenzy, to the
                                                    mountain,

---

972 PENTHEUS' "renown" will presumably be as a figure of myth, a
     deluded victim rather than a hero.

974 It has been maintained by some critics that the description of
     PENTHEUS as a "youth" prepares the audience for a shift of
     sympathy toward him in the scenes that follow. This is im-
     probable: "the youth" bears some emphasis, but not so much
     as would be needed to give this neutral word a definitely sym-
     pathetic colouring. The shift-of-sympathy idea will be further
     discussed in the note on 1121.

977– The Fourth Stasimon is a song of furious vengeance, although
1023   it contains one passage of moralizing reflection that recalls
       parts of the two preceding odes. In form it resembles the Third
       Stasimon: strophe and antistrophe, each with a refrain, then a
       brief epode. It is distinguished from it by metre, here pre-
       dominantly "dochmiac." The basic measure is ∪ − − ∪ −, but
       this can be varied, notably by the resolution of a long syllable
       into two shorts. Dochmiacs were used to express excitement
       and strong emotion, either joy or sorrow or, as here, rage and
       determination. Indeed it is the last of these that is best sug-
       gested by a succession of pure dochmiacs, which produce a
       somewhat jerky and ponderous effect; but this is tempered by
       an increase in the number of short syllables.

       After summoning the spirit of Frenzy to fill the women on
       Cithaeron with vengeful madness, the CHORUS imagine the

where the daughters of Cadmus have their
sacred band;
goad them in madness
against the man dressed up as a woman, 980
the frenzied spy on the maenads.
His mother first from smooth cliff

---

discovery of PENTHEUS by AGAUE. The antistrophe recalls his vicious impiety and expounds the dangers of failing to honour the gods. The twice-sung refrain is savage in its hatred for PENTHEUS and its desire for his blood; and the epode matches the opening invocation by summoning DIONYSUS as animal and as hunter.

Poetically this is one of the least interesting of the odes of *The Bacchae;* yet it has a stark, almost Aeschylean quality that gives it strong dramatic force.

977 *Frenzy:* the Greek name is *Lyssa*—a frightful figure associated with the Erinyes, or Avenging Furies—who hunts down her victims with hounds. In a way the maenads, addressed by AGAUE at 731 as "my coursing hounds," are to become the Furies' human embodiment.

981 *the frenzied spy:* the CHORUS knows that PENTHEUS is already possessed, so their chief concern now is that the maenads will be ready for him.

982– It is true that the choral song covers the time during which
990 PENTHEUS meets his death; yet their imagining of events leading up to it is not an act of second sight, since it does not accord with what actually happens as the MESSENGER will describe it at 1073ff. There PENTHEUS is sighted by all the maenads together (1095) as he is lifted on the treetop; there is no question of AGAUE standing on a cliff, as here, and seeing him "lurking" (984), and then calling to the other women. In fact this version is a development of what the first MESSENGER from Cithaeron had reported about a quite separate but intentionally parallel incident: AGAUE's coming across the cowherd in ambush, her cry to the women "O my coursing

or *pinnacle shall see him*
lurking, and shall call to the maenads:
    "Who is this tracker   985
of the Cadmeian mountain-runners that has
        come, has come,
to the mountain, the mountain, O bac-
    chants? Who can have given him
        birth?
    For not from blood
of women is he sprung, but from some
        lioness
or from Libyan gorgons is his descent!"   990

Let Vengeance go forth manifest, let her go bearing the
        sword,
    butchering through the throat
    Echion's ungodly, unlawful, unrighteous,   995
        earth-born offspring,

---

hounds, we are hunted by these men; but follow me, follow . . . ," and the subsequent tearing to pieces of the cattle
(728ff.). Thus the CHORUS describes the *sort of thing* they
hope and believe will happen; actually it does not happen
quite like that, mainly because the god takes advantage of
PENTHEUS' desire to climb the tree (1061); but by harking
back, quite naturally, to the attack on the cowherd and shepherds the CHORUS gives a gruesome hint of the nature of
PENTHEUS' destruction.

987– AGAUE uses a common trope to express the spy's inhumanity,
990   but there is of course a special irony in "who can have given
    him birth?" (because she did) and "from some lioness" (be-
    cause at 1174 she will think PENTHEUS' head is that of a young
    lion).

995f *Echion's . . . earth-born offspring:* compare 538–44—the
    theme of PENTHEUS' monstrous and inhuman nature continues
    that of the Second Stasimon.

ANTISTROPHE 1

who with unrighteous judgment and lawless tem-
                                        per
against your secret worship, Bacchic one, and your
                                        mother's,
    with maddened cunning
and crazed spirit sallies forth   1000
as though to subdue by force that which cannot be
                                        conquered.
As a chastisement of judgments, death accepts
    no excuses with regard to things divine;
and to behave as a mortal means a life free from
                                        grief.

    Wisdom I do not grudge—   1005

1002– This part of the antistrophe is complicated, and was evidently
1010 too much for the copyists in places. The general sense is not in
doubt; my translation is based on Gilbert Murray's *Oxford
Classical Text*, but with Dodds' *sophronism'* at 1002 and
something like *hōs agein* at 1007. Once again, as in the
First and particularly the Third Stasimon, the CHORUS urges
a life of moderation and piety; the fatal consequences of the
opposite are stressed; but the fury of the refrain is in even
sharper contrast with the quiet and philosophical tone of
1005–10 than the moralizing of this CHORUS usually is with
some of its ritual behaviour. For specific reminiscences of earlier odes compare 1002f. with 884–87, 1005–7 with 877–897,
1008f. with 425f., 1009f. with 890–94.

1002f The meaning is that false judgments about the gods are punished by death, and death accepts no excuses.

1005f The punctuation is uncertain here, but in any case the
CHORUS pays lip service to wisdom, *sophon*, and goes on to
declare that other things are more important as a guide to
conduct.

I delight in hunting it down, but the other things
                                                   are great
and manifest, and so lead life to what is fair:
          by day and into the night
to be pure and reverent, and, casting out customs
that lie outside justice, to honour the gods.   1010

Let Vengeance go forth manifest, let her go bearing the
                                              sword,
          butchering through the throat
               Echion's ungodly, unlawful, unrighteous,   1015
               earth-born offspring.

EPODE

Appear as a bull or a many-headed
snake or a fire-blazing lion to behold!
   Go, O Bacchus—around the hunter of
                                   bacchants 1020
     with smiling face cast your noose;

1017f The god is summoned in one of his animal, and therefore
     wildest, forms; the snake is described as a monstrous one (like
     the Hydra) to make it frightening—cf. note on 102–4.

1020– Suddenly DIONYSUS becomes hunter (continuing the meta-
1023 phor of 848 and elsewhere), not animal. The switch empha-
     sizes his duality and his many forms. It is now the maenads
     who are animal, a "deadly herd" in 1022; they are being hunted
     by PENTHEUS (1020), who will be outhunted by DIONYSUS,
     and unlike the herd of cattle that they tore to pieces earlier,
     they will become a deadly herd through the god and will tear
     to pieces their hunter (see also pp. 13f.). The "smiling face"
     of 1021 recalls the smiling captive of 439, and the CHORUS
     unconsciously identifies the demeanour of the god in his true
     and his disguised form.

109

under the deadly herd
of maenads let him fall!

Enter a messenger from Cithaeron.

SECOND MESSENGER   *O house that once was fortunate in the*
sight of Hellas,
descended from the old man of Sidon who sowed in the earth   1025
the earth-born crop of the serpent, the snake,
how I mourn for you—a slave, but still I mourn!   1027

CHORUS   *What is it? Have you news to tell us from the*
bacchants?   1029

SECOND MESSENGER   *Pentheus is destroyed, the son of*
Echion!   1030

1024– *Scene 5* After an initial exchange between the MESSENGER
1152   and the jubilant CHORUS the whole scene is taken up by
       his report of PENTHEUS' death at the hands of the women
       on Cithaeron. The CHORUS had called for bloody vengeance,
       and, even as they sang, it was being achieved. The fact
       of PENTHEUS' death was expected; only the manner was
       not entirely clear, and all the earlier hints are realized in the
       careful and graphic description of the ultimate *sparagmos*.
       The enthusiasm of AGAUE and her equally maddened sisters
       and companions knows no bounds, and from now on the
       tragedy is to be hers and theirs as much as PENTHEUS'. His
       death is what the play has been inexorably tending toward, but
       now the survivors are left to work out the consequences, gather
       up the bloodstained and scattered remains, and assess respon-
       sibilities—if they can.

1024– The oblique approach, with its sinister "once", is typical of
1027   tragic messengers. The "old man of Sidon" is CADMUS (note on
       171f.); the serpent-snake is the dragon who guarded the spring
       of Ares, who was slain by CADMUS, and whose teeth were
       sown. The emphasis on a slave's capacity for loyalty is typically
       Euripidean.

CHORUS
> O lord Bromios, you are revealed
> as a mighty god!

SECOND MESSENGER What do you mean? What is this you said? Do you really rejoice,
woman, over my masters' ill fortune?

CHORUS
> I cry in ecstasy, a foreigner, in
> my alien strains,
> for no longer do I cringe under
> fear of imprisonment. 1035

SECOND MESSENGER Do you judge the Thebans so feeble . . .

      *   *   *   *   *   *

CHORUS
> Dionysus, Dionysus, not Thebes
> has power over me!

SECOND MESSENGER We must make allowances for you—except it is not good
to rejoice, women, over the accomplishment of evil. 1040

CHORUS
> Tell me, explain—with what
> doom did he die,
> the man unjust, injustice's con-
> triver?

SECOND MESSENGER When we had left the outlying farms of this Theban land
and gone beyond the streams of Asopus
we were striking into the uplands of Cithaeron, 1045
Pentheus and I—for I was following my master—
and the stranger who was escort in our mission.

1031 At this point, and until 1042, in its joy at the news, the CHORUS responds in excited dochmiacs (note on 977–1023).

1036 The verse is incomplete, and probably another whole verse has been lost too; the required sense is "that they will not punish you for this display of joy."

Well, first we take up position in a grassy valley,
keeping silence both in our movements and in respect of speech
that we may see without being seen.   1050
There was a glen enclosed by cliffs, with water running through,
overshadowed by pines, where the maenads
were seated, occupying their hands in pleasant tasks.
Some of them were re-garlanding with trailing ivy
a thyrsus that had come to pieces;   1055
others, like foals released from the painted yoke,
were chanting in antiphon a bacchic song.
But the wretched Pentheus, since he could not see the throng
     of women,
spoke these words: "Stranger, where we stand
my vision does not reach the spurious maenads;   1060
but on the cliffs, by climbing into a lofty fir,
I could properly see the maenads' shameful deeds."
The next thing, I see from the stranger this miracle:
taking hold of a fir tree's topmost, skyward branch,
he drew it down, down, down to the dark ground;   1065
it was curved like a bow—or as a rounded wheel,

1048 This *grassy valley* is not the same as the cliff-enclosed glen or
      defile of 1051, which seems to cut through it.

1051 *with water running through* represents a prominent and suc-
      cessful onomatopoeia in the Greek: hŭdăsĭ dĭăbrŏchŏn, where
      the succession of seven short syllables, unusual for iambic
      verse, undoubtedly imitates the sound of trickling water.

1056 *painted*: an evocative word that adds to the idea of lightness
      and gaiety, or more strictly of release and freedom.

1065 *down, down, down*: another unusually emphatic onomato-
      poeia, katēgen, ēgen, ēgen in Greek.

1066f A simile whose meaning has often been discussed. A popular
      view at present is that it describes a pole lathe, in which a
      wheel is turned by the continuous bending and releasing of a
      flexible spar. The image would be exact but rather complicated
      and not at all easy to reconcile with the Greek text; moreover

when its outline is traced by the compass, extends its circuit.
So the stranger drew down with his hands the mountain trunk
and bent it to the earth, performing deeds that were not mortal;
and seating Pentheus on the fir branches   1070
he let the young tree upright, passing it through his hands
without shaking it, taking care not to unseat him.
Upright it towered right into the upper air
with my master seated on its back—
he was seen by, rather than saw, the maenads!   1075
For just as he was coming into sight on his lofty seat
(and the stranger was no longer to be seen)
from the upper air a voice—Dionysus

---

such devices, though possible enough, are not otherwise at-
tested in ancient Greece. I suspect that the key word *tornōi*
simply has its commonest and basic meaning of "compass" (as
in the translation), or more precisely a peg-and-line for mark-
ing out a circle. A familiar use would be for outlining wheel
rims or solid wheels to be cut from timber; half the circuit, at
least, of the wheel's outline would be traced in the way the
tree was drawn down: ∩ . Yet this, too, it must be ad-
mitted, seems needlessly complex and tortuously expressed—
though this may be due simply to our ignorance.

1070   PENTHEUS' mounting of the tree may be a traditional element
in the myth—another of DIONYSUS' victims, Erigone, hanged
herself from a tree according to a definitely old story (see also
Dodds, *ad loc.*). That the tree was connected with primitive
ritual, as J. G. Frazer thought, is possible but no more, and
there is really nothing in particular to suggest it; see also the
note on 1096ff. There are plenty of purely narrative reasons for
the tree and the consequent bombardment: PENTHEUS' desire
to see more clearly, the opportunity for a further miracle in
the bending of the tree, PENTHEUS' helplessness and absurdity
when stranded there, the suspense when the maenads are at
first unable to reach him.

1078–   This is the second time the invisible god has given utterance,
1081   the first being when he rallied his true bacchants and called

as one may guess—cried out: "Maidens,
I bring the man who makes you and me and my worship   1080
into a mockery: take revenge on him!"
Just as these words were uttered, between sky
and earth extended a glow of holy fire.
The air of heaven was silent, in silence the wooded glade
held its leaves, of wild creatures you would have heard no cry.   1085
And they, who had not perceived the sound distinctly,
stood up and turned their eyes this way and that.
Again he commanded them; and when Cadmus' daughters
recognized the order, now plainly heard, of the Bacchic god,
they darted off, their feet carrying them   1090
with the speed of a dove as they ran at full stretch—
Agaue, Pentheus' mother, and her blood sisters

---

down fire and earthquake on the palace (576ff.). There is a
possible resemblance to the divine voice that summons Oedipus in Sophocles' roughly contemporary play *Oedipus at
Colonus*, 1621ff.

1082f Again, as when the divine voice was heard before, there is a
supernatural increase of light. Then, the fire by Semele's tomb
blazed up; now there is something like a flash of lightning, but
one that seems more than momentary. DIONYSUS was, in fact,
occasionally imagined as making lightning, probably because of
his first birth through the lightning that struck Semele (3).
A glow of fire regularly indicates a divine presence (as with
Demeter in *Homeric Hymn* II, 189) or divine inspiration (as
with god-favoured heroes in *The Iliad*).

1084f The divine voice, the blaze of fire, now silence; this silence is
caused, presumably, partly by the ceasing of the voice, partly
(if *aither*, here translated as "air of heaven," may loosely ex-
tend to air in general as at 1099) by the stilling of all wind.
The silence of Nature in the presence of a god became a theme
of later poetry, but it is not clear how familiar it was before
Euripides. This silence and the stillness crystallize the scene:
over there PENTHEUS in the fir tree, here in the glen the
maenads, and everywhere the mysterious glow.

and all the bacchants. Through the torrented glade
and broken rocks they leaped, crazed by the inspiration of the
    god.
When they saw my master seated on the fir tree,   1095
first of all they hurled stones at him
with all their strength, climbing the facing tower of rock,
and he was bombarded, too, with branches of fir.
Others discharged their thyrsi through the air
at Pentheus, an unhappy aiming—but did not reach him;   1100
he was too high even for their ardour
as he sat there in misery, overtaken by helplessness.
In the end they pounded at the roots with branches of oak

1095 The maenads' first sighting of PENTHEUS is mentioned very briefly, almost perfunctorily—it is quite different from the scene imagined by the CHORUS at 982–90 (see note).

1096ff Stoning was sometimes a ritual act, for example to drive out of a city a polluted man or animal, and Dodds thinks that the bombardment of PENTHEUS may be a ritual survival (see also note on 1070). On the other hand it is perfectly natural to throw things at someone who needs to be dislodged from a tree—indeed the ritual act itself was merely a formalization of what would be best in particular circumstances. In short, if you want to make sure of driving someone away without much risk of either touching or killing him, stones are best. One argument for ritual origin can be rejected: the stoning does not seem "below the level of tragedy" (Dodds) to most readers, as I would guess; and even if it did to some, that would tell us nothing about its effect on a Greek audience or the possible motive for it in the mind of the playwright.

1103f The received text means literally "striking branches of oak as though with a thunderbolt they tried . . . ," which would imply that they first split off branches and then used them as levers. I prefer to envisage a minute change in the words for "branches of oak," from the accusative case to the dative, so that both verses describe the same action; for the splitting of oak branches is a little odd, and the unusual verb, with its un-

115

and tried to tear them up with levers not of iron;
but when all their efforts accomplished no result,   1105
Agaue said: "Come, stand round in a circle
and grasp the sapling, maenads, to capture
the mounted beast and prevent his reporting the god's
secret dances." Then they applied countless hands
to the fir tree, and dragged it out of the earth.   1110
Sitting on high, from high he is hurled down
and falls to the ground with countless groans—
Pentheus; for he was beginning to understand that he was close
      to ruin.
First his mother started the slaughter as priestess
and falls upon him; he hurled away the snood   1115
from his hair, for the wretched Agaue to recognize
and not kill him—and says, touching
her cheek, "Look, it is I, mother, your child
Pentheus, whom you bore in the house of Echion!
Take pity on me, mother, and do not by reason of my   1120
errors murder your own child!"

---

doubtedly strong sense, is better related to the main action of
trying to lever up the tree rather than to a mere preliminary.

1108   The *mounted beast* is still a metaphor; AGAUE recognizes him
       as a man, though a monstrous one, but by 1141f. probably and
       1174 certainly she thinks he is a lion.

1113   Again the etymological connection of "Pentheus" with
       "mourning"; cf. 367 and note, and 508.

1114   The *sparagmos* is treated as a ritual act, and ritual acts are
       carried out or initiated by a priest or priestess.

1120f Too much emphasis has been placed on this passage, even by
       a sensible critic like Dodds, who writes (on pp. 216f. of his
       commentary) that "Pentheus dies sane . . . and repentant.
       . . . His repentance must be taken as sincere." This implies
       that PENTHEUS is now completely free not only of his recent
       delusions but also of his longer-standing attitude toward
       DIONYSUS, and that he sees the whole of his folly. Yet the

116

But she, discharging foam from her mouth and rolling
her eyes all round, her mind not as it should be,
was possessed by the Bacchic god; and her son did not persuade
  her.
Grasping his left arm below the elbow   1125
and setting her foot against the unhappy man's ribs,
she tore his shoulder out, not by her normal strength,

Greek word translated as *errors* in 1121 (*hamartiaisi*) can imply anything from simple mistakes of judgment to definite sins of commission. Here I think it most likely that the sense lies between these extremes—something like "failings." PEN-THEUS' appeal to his mother is certainly more to the point than his recent actions have been; to that extent terror has brought back sanity. But is he yet completely sane? Does he see the truth of the whole situation? We do not know, but it seems improbable. And does the mere mention of the ambiguous "errors" imply all that is meant by "sincere repentance" (even when the phrase is stripped of its Christian overtones)? PEN-THEUS sees that he has made mistakes, that things have gone drastically wrong; that is certain. He probably also sees that his whole idea of dressing up, of spying on the women, was misguided; and some of the warnings of the CHORUS, the stranger, and the MESSENGERS may flash through his mind. We should not allow modern fantasies about "moments of truth" to persuade us that more than this was likely or intended by the playwright.

1122f The description is equally clinical in the Greek; the symptoms are those of epilepsy, known to the Greeks as "the sacred dis-ease" because of its similarity to certain forms of religious in-spiration.

1124 The "possession" was not, of course, a normal one for a bac-chant, although the symptoms were an exaggerated form of some of the normal ones.

1127f The Dionysiac excess of strength here reaches its macabre climax (cf. note on 945-54).

but the god gave a special ease to her hands.
Ino was wrecking the other side of him,
breaking his flesh, and Autonoe and the whole mob   1130
of bacchants laid hold on him; all gave voice at once—
he moaning with what breath was left in him,
they screaming in triumph. One was carrying a forearm,
another a foot with the boot still on; his ribs
were being laid bare by the tearing; and each of the women, with
    hands   1135
all bloody, was playing ball with Pentheus' flesh.
    The body lies scattered, part under harsh
rocks, part among the deep-wooded foliage of the forest,
no easy search; and the poor head,
which his mother just then seized in her hands,   1140
she fixed on the point of her thyrsus, and as if it belonged
to a mountain lion she carries it right across Cithaeron,
leaving her sisters among the maenad-dancers.
She passes, rejoicing in her ill-fated spoils,
within these walls, calling on the Bacchic god   1145
as fellow hunter, fellow worker in the kill,
triumphant victor—but for her he brings tears as victory!
    So I shall depart, out of the way of this calamity,
before Agaue approaches the palace.
To be of sound mind and reverence the things divine   1150
is finest—and I think it is also the wisest
practice for mortal men to follow.

1137ff The emphasis on the scattering of the body and AGAUE's
treatment of the head prepares the way for the next scene.

1150– A simple moralization is common enough at the end of a
1152 speech reporting disaster, but here the form is significant; the
MESSENGER restates the CHORUS' final answer to its constant
question about the nature of wisdom (note on 877–81). 1151f.
means literally "the wisest practice for mortals, for those who
practise it," a mild and insignificant word-play that would
become misleadingly conspicuous in any attempted English
rendering.

CHORUS   *Let us dance to the Bacchic god,*
let us shout aloud the disaster
of the dragon's descendant, Pentheus;   1155
who took female raiment
and the fennel-rod, Hades' pledge,
in its thyrsus-shape
with a bull to lead him into disaster.
Cadmeian bacchants,   1160
you have made your victory song a famous
                              one—
to end in wailing, in tears!
A fine contest, to embrace your child
with a hand dripping with blood!

1153– *Fifth Stasimon*: In the urgency of the moment there is only
1164   time for a very short song, primarily dochmiac in rhythm
(note on 977–1023). In its first half the CHORUS triumphs
over PENTHEUS' death, consistent with its mood in the preceding stasimon; in the second half it turns to the horror of what
the pseudo-bacchants have accomplished.

1157   *Hades' pledge*: most editors try to amend the word meaning
"pledge," unnecessarily, I think. The meaning is that PEN-
THEUS' taking of the thyrsus and his disguise as a bacchant
guaranteed his death.

1158   *in its thyrsus-shape*: literally "well-thyrsused," an untranslat-
able term, implying no more than that the fennel-rod had
been well made into a thyrsus.

1159   *with a bull*: see 920f., where PENTHEUS saw the stranger as a
bull—hardly a delusion, but rather a true glimpse of the animal
nature of the god in his wildest and most potent form.

1160– There is sorrow, irony, and some disapproval in these verses
1164   and those that follow; but does the CHORUS totally condemn
the Theban women, or is their maenadism, "spurious" though
it is, something of a bond?

1161– *victory song . . . fine contest*: conscious references to 1147,
1163   975, 964.

But I see hastening to the palace   1165
Pentheus' mother Agaue, her eyes
rolling; so prepare to welcome the revellers of the god of ecstasy!

STROPHE

AGAUE   Bacchants of Asia—

CHORUS   Why do you rouse me, O?

AGAUE   I bring from the mountains
                        a freshly cut tendril to these halls,   1170
                            a happy hunting!

CHORUS   I see it, and shall accept you as a fellow reveller.

1165–   All that follows the final stasimon was known as the *Exodos*,
1392   the "end" or "issue" of the drama (which culminates in the
        literal "going out" of the CHORUS). PENTHEUS is dead, and the
        issue of *The Bacchae* is concerned with AGAUE's madness and
        gradual recognition of herself and her actions, with laments
        for the murdered man, and with the revelation by the god of
        punishments for the guilty, followed by further lamentations.

1168–   The rapid conversation between AGAUE, mad and triumphant,
1199   and the CHORUS, impatient and humouring by turns, is sung in
        two corresponding stanzas, mainly dochmiac in rhythm (see
        note on 977–1023). The constant and apparently pointless in-
        terruptions, particularly at 1177 and 1182, exemplify a tragic
        convention for showing excitement or impatience and would
        seem less stylized and more natural in performance than they
        do in print.

1170   *tendril*: the Greek word means anything shaped like a spiral—
        here, presumably, a curling shoot of ivy. The "lion's" head that
        AGAUE carries on her thyrsus-point (1141f.), with its "crest of
        soft hair" (1186), is described as though it were the ivy that
        was ordinarily fastened to the thyrsus-tip. Whether this is
        metaphor or delusion remains ambiguous.

1172   The CHORUS' implied acceptance of AGAUE is ironical (also
        1180).

120

AGAUE	*I caught this without snares—*
	a savage lion's young whelp,
	as can be seen. 1175
CHORUS	*From what wild spot?*
AGAUE	*Cithaeron . . .*
CHORUS	*Cithaeron?*
AGAUE	*. . . slew him.*
CHORUS	*Who struck the blow?*
AGAUE	*Mine was the privilege first.*
CHORUS	*Happy Agaue . . .*
AGAUE	*. . . is what I am called in the*
	sacred bands! 1180
CHORUS	*Who else?*
AGAUE	*Of Cadmus . . .*
CHORUS	*What of Cadmus?*
AGAUE	*. . . the offspring*
	after me, after me laid
	hands on this beast; a fortunate quarry indeed!

ANTISTROPHE

AGAUE	*Partake then of the feast!*
CHORUS	*What, partake, poor wretch?*

1184 *What, partake, poor wretch?*: the CHORUS is shocked by the
suggestion of eating the head (a suggestion that is not renewed, see note on 1242), though it soon reverts to humouring
AGAUE. There are two or three hints in later Greek sources that
on rare occasions bacchants tore and tasted a human victim,
but the practice was clearly irregular and would arouse repul-
sion in ordinary worshippers.

121

AGAUE	*The bull is a young one—* *beneath the crest of soft hair, his jaw* *sprouts with fresh down.*	1185
CHORUS	*Yes, he looks like a beast of the open country, by* *his locks.*	
AGAUE	*The Bacchic huntsman* *wisely, cleverly swung his maenads* *upon this beast.*	1190
CHORUS	*For our lord is a hunter.*	
AGAUE	*You praise me?*	
CHORUS	*I praise you.*	
AGAUE	*Soon the Cadmeians . . .*	1194
CHORUS	*and your child Pentheus, too . . .*	
AGAUE	*shall praise his mother . . .*	
CHORUS	*for catching the quarry . . .*	
AGAUE	*this lion-natured one . . .*	
CHORUS	*a special one . . .*	
AGAUE	*in a special way!*	
CHORUS	*You exult in it?*	

1185 The word translated "bull," literally bullock, is also sometimes applied to other young animals, so it is not certain that AGAUE strays at this point from her otherwise consistent delusion, during this whole conversation, that what she is holding is the head of a young lion.

1197 *special*: the same word in Greek as was applied to the "superior" men from whom the CHORUS recoiled at 429; its basic meaning is "exceptional," "odd." That Euripides was aware of the significance of the repetition may be confirmed by the next note.

AGAUE   *I am overjoyed;*
                          great things have I
                achieved, great and manifest for this land.

CHORUS *Show, then, poor woman, to the citizens*   **1200**
your victorious plunder, which you have carried here.

AGAUE   *O you who dwell in the fair-towered town*
of the Theban land, come and see this quarry,
the beast which we daughters of Cadmus have hunted down—
not with the Thessalians' thonged missiles,   **1205**
not with nets, but with the cutting edge
of our own fair hands. After this need one boast
about owning the useless products of spear-makers?
We with unaided hands both caught this beast
and tore his limbs apart.   **1210**
Where is my old father? Let him come near.
And where is my child Pentheus? Let him raise up
the steps of joinered ladders against the building,
to nail on the beam ends this lion's

1199 *great and manifest:* these are the very terms applied by the
CHORUS at 1006f. to the idea of being pure and reverent! It is
conceivable that the phrase is simply a cult formula, but more
likely that the repetition is deliberate. If so, the irony is intense:
the CHORUS evades complicated questions of "wisdom" and
concentrates on what is manifest, namely, moderation and
piety; but AGAUE's conception of what is manifest entails the
murder of her son.

1200ff The CHORUS addresses AGAUE pityingly and she responds like
an automaton, holding up her trophy for the citizens of
Thebes.

1205 *thonged missiles:* throwing spears often had loops for the
fingers halfway down their shafts. Thessaly was noted for its
spears and spearsmen.

1207f The pompous form of this statement accords with AGAUE's
mood of manic conceit: spears are unnecessary utensils, and
conventional hunters have no cause for boasting.

1214 *beam ends:* literally "triglyphs," the technical word for the

head, which I have hunted and brought here.   1215

Enter CADMUS, with servants carrying a covered litter.

CADMUS   Follow me, bearing the sad weight
of Pentheus, follow, my servants, in front of the palace;
whose body, after laborious and endless search,
I am bringing—I found it in the glens of Cithaeron
shredded in pieces, and got nothing in the same spot,   1220
but it lay scattered in the tangled woods.
For I heard from someone of my daughters' shameless deeds,
back in the town, when I had passed within the walls
with old Tiresias, coming from the bacchants;
and turning back to the mountain I recovered   1225
my son who died at the hands of the maenads.
And I saw her who bore Actaeon to Aristaeus,

---

triple fluting that disguised or decorated the ends of the longi-
tudinal roof beams in a formal building. Here the plural is
generic, and indicates "along the line of the beam ends."

1216f Just as the audience is digesting the fact that PENTHEUS is
unavailable to nail up his own head, CADMUS enters from
Cithaeron carrying the rest of him—a neat if minor *coup de
théâtre*.

1224 *coming from the bacchants*: so CADMUS and TIRESIAS did reach
Cithaeron and do some dancing. Therefore the rites were not
entirely "secret" (as AGAUE had claimed at 1109), and what
the maenads objected to was being spied on rather than being
joined by sincere male participants.

1227f Actaeon, son of Autonoe and Aristaeus, was therefore
nephew of AGAUE and first cousin to PENTHEUS. He was torn
to pieces by his own hounds for offending a deity (Artemis,
whom he claimed to excel in hunting); he is therefore both
precursor and paradigm for PENTHEUS, and had already been
cited as a warning by CADMUS (337–40 and note). Moreover
his *sparagmos*, likewise, took place on Mount Cithaeron
(1291f.).

Autonoe, and Ino with her,
still struck with frenzy, poor women, among the thickets;
but she, someone told me, with bacchic step   1230
was on her way here, Agaue; nor were we misinformed,
for I see her—and it is not a happy sight.

AGAUE   Father, you can make the proudest of boasts,
that you have begotten by far the best daughters
of all mortals. I mean all of us, but especially myself,   1235
who have left behind the shuttles by the looms
and come to something greater—hunting wild beasts with my
        hands!
I bear in my arms, as you see, this
proof of valour that I have caught, that it may be hung
against your palace. You, father, take it in your hands;   1240
rejoice in my hunting and
invite your friends to a feast; for you are blessed,
blessed, since we have achieved such things!

CADMUS   O sorrow unmeasurable and beyond seeing,
since murder you have achieved with those poor hands!   1245
A fine victim you have struck down for the gods—
and invite Thebes here, and me, to the feast!
Alas for misfortune—first for yours, then mine;
how the god has ruined us, justly, but to excess,

1239f *hung:* the Greek verb is especially used for dedicatory offerings
        hung on the walls of temples.

1242   The "lion's" head is to be hung up—therefore AGAUE does not
        mean it to be consumed at the feast, in contrast to her sugges-
        tion to the CHORUS at 1184.

1244   CADMUS' first words to his daughter may have subtle over-
        tones: the Greek word for "sorrow" here is *penthos;* its con-
        nection with PENTHEUS was stressed at 367, 508, and 1113; and
        this sorrow is "immeasurable" and "beyond seeing," like PEN-
        THEUS' body which CADMUS has had to gather with (liter-
        ally) "countless searchings" (1218).

1249f This is CADMUS' unwavering reaction to the disaster: DIONY-

the lord Bromios who is our kinsman!   1250

AGAUE   *How bad-tempered is old age among men*
and scowling in its looks! Would that my child
were a successful hunter, made like his mother in his ways,
whenever in company with the young Thebans
he went after beasts! But fighting against gods   1255
is all he can do. He must be rebuked, father,
by you. Who will call him here into my sight
to see my happiness?

CADMUS   *Alas! if you all realize what you have done*
you will grieve with a dreadful grief; but if to the end   1260
you persist in your present condition,
though far from fortunate, you will think you are free from
   misfortune.

---

sus was justified in exacting punishment, but the punishment is too severe (cf. 1346). In saying "the god has ruined *us* justly" he accepts a portion, at least, of the responsibility, even though he and TIRESIAS did not resist the god. Or had they done so, at first, and were their bacchic prancings part of the god's revenge (cf. notes on 186–90 and 1360–62)? Or does he rather recognize that his reasons for accepting DIONYSUS—to preserve the family reputation—were the wrong ones? And yet he seems to dwell on this theme even here, in the words "who is our kinsman."

1251–   To boastfulness AGAUE now adds a petulant resentment at the
1258   lack of obvious approval. There is a possible implication in her words that PENTHEUS was not generally distinguished as a man of action, which might suit the theory of his effeminate nature; but perhaps she merely despises anyone who cannot kill with bare hands.

1259–   The rather artificial antithesis (of which the point is that re-
1262   covery means grief, so much so that staying mad might be almost worth it) is deliberately cryptic, enough at least to arouse a suspicion in AGAUE that all is not well.

AGAUE What is not good, what is painful in this?

CADMUS (pointing) First turn your gaze on this sky above.

AGAUE There: why did you suggest I look at it? 1265

CADMUS Is it the same, or does it seem to you to be changing?

AGAUE It is brighter than before and shines with a holier light.

CADMUS And is this passionate excitement still in your heart?

AGAUE I do not understand this question—and yet I am somehow becoming
in my full senses, changed from my previous state of mind. 1270

CADMUS So you could understand a question and give a plain answer?

AGAUE Yes, for I have indeed forgotten what we said before, father.

1264ff Ten years or so before The Bacchae Euripides had written another great scene of madness and recovery in his Heracles, which also survives. Heracles' actual process of recovery (he had killed his wife and children while mad) is more rapid than AGAUE's; but there is a long stichomythia (1113ff.) in which he is led by his father Amphitryon to recognize just what he has done. This is quite similar in outline to AGAUE's anagnorisis (to use Aristotle's well-known term for the "recognition," whether of the true situation or of an actual person, which he thought essential in a good tragedy); but it is quite different in detail and less refined in its psychological insight.

1269f The break in the series of single-verse utterances marks a particularly crucial moment, here as in other of Euripides' plays. It is possible, as Dodds suggests, that there is a pause after 1269; CADMUS, instead of speaking or interrupting, hangs on AGAUE's words.

CADMUS   To what household did you go at your marriage?

AGAUE   You gave me to one of the Sown Men, Echion, as they say.

CADMUS   So what child was born for your husband in his home?   1275

AGAUE   Pentheus, through my union with his father.

CADMUS   Whose head, then, are you holding in your arms?

AGAUE   A lion's—at least, so the women hunters said.

CADMUS   Now consider truly—looking costs little trouble.

AGAUE   (violently agitated)   Ah, what do I see? What is this I am carrying in my hands?   1280

CADMUS   Look hard at it and understand more clearly.

AGAUE   What I see is grief, deep grief, and misery for me!

CADMUS   It does not seem to you to resemble a lion?

AGAUE   No, but it is Pentheus' head I am holding, unhappy woman!

CADMUS   Yes, Pentheus', bewailed before you recognized him!   1285

AGAUE   Who killed him? How did he come into my hands?

CADMUS   Unhappy truth, how hard you are to tell at this moment!

1273f CADMUS' circuitous approach to AGAUE's recognition of her own identity is sensible in itself and well observed; but the "Sown Men" detail is not strictly necessary and could be intended by Euripides to remind the audience of the significance of PENTHEUS' unusual ancestry, which renders him, in one way, similar to DIONYSUS (p. 15). The phrase "as they say" reflects AGAUE's caution—or it is a pure convention of diction; it surely does not (as Dodds suggests) indicate any doubt on AGAUE's part about the story of the Sown Men.

AGAUE *Speak, since my heart sinks at what is to come!*

CADMUS *You killed him, you and your sisters.*

AGAUE *But where did he die? At home? Or whereabouts?* 1290

CADMUS *Where previously the hounds divided out Actaeon.*

AGAUE *But why did he come to Cithaeron, this ill-starred man?*

CADMUS *He meant to jeer at the god, and your bacchic rites, by going there.*

AGAUE *And we—in what manner did we alight there?*

CADMUS *You were made mad, and the whole land was possessed by bacchic frenzy.* 1295

AGAUE *Dionysus destroyed us, now I realize it!*

1291 Another significant allusion to PENTHEUS' family connections; see note on 1227f.

1295 *made mad:* the verb of itself need imply little more than the one applied in this same verse to the land as a whole, *possessed by bacchic frenzy,* or more literally, "made thoroughly bacchic." Yet although the CHORUS can address itself as "maenads," literally "maddened women," there *is* a distinction, in this play at least, between the terminology for normal and for abnormal Dionysiac possession. Thus forms of the verb "to madden" are reserved for the previously recalcitrant Theban women; the CHORUS never describes itself by such verbs, which it reserves for "madmen" like PENTHEUS who are rebuked for excess (e.g., 400, 887, 999); only the Satyrs, among more or less complimentary references, are "maddened" or "ecstatic" at 130. Of course the meaning does verge into that of "ecstatic," but in the present verse something more drastic is clearly meant.

1296 Compare for example *Hippolytus* 1401 for the formal recognition, by the victim, of the deity who has been offended and so caused the suffering.

CADMUS Yes, since he was subjected to insult; for you did not consider him a god.

AGAUE And the beloved body of my son, where is it, father?

CADMUS I searched it out with difficulty, and am carrying it here.

AGAUE Is it all fitted together in decent fashion, limb to limb?   1300

·   ·   ·   ·   ·   ·

[a long passage is missing here]

1300 Something is clearly missing after this verse; we must envisage a lacuna (not in the surviving manuscript—there is only a single one for the latter part of the play—but in some ancestor) of more than a single verse, since CADMUS' answer to the question in 1300 would be "no" and could not simply lead on to 1301. Moreover there is another and even more striking lacuna between 1329 and 1330, where the end of AGAUE's sentence and the whole beginning of the god's prophecy are missing. Now an ancient summary of the end of the play shows roughly what went into one of these gaps. The third-century A.D. rhetorical writer Apsines, discussing means of arousing pity, reports that "Agaue, rid of her madness and recognizing that her own child has been torn to pieces, accuses herself . . . holding each of his [viz. Pentheus'] limbs in her hands she laments in accordance with each of them." Most scholars, including Wilamowitz, Murray, and Dodds, have thought that AGAUE's lament and presumed reassembly of the limbs belong in the second gap, somewhere after 1329; but I believe, as did C. Robert, that they more probably came after 1300. This gives an immediate sequence, as implied by Apsines, between AGAUE's recognition and her laments; it leads on naturally from her inquiry about the body at 1298 and 1300; and CADMUS' lamentations, especially 1308ff., where he directly addresses PENTHEUS, are more appropriate if the body has already been

130

AGAUE   *What portion of my folly attached itself to Pentheus?* 1301

---

decently reassembled. Moreover his closing survey of the disaster and his moralizing over it, at 1323–26, seem to lead more naturally to the epiphany of the god than to further lamentations. (Dodds' two arguments against Robert, on p. 232 of his commentary, do not seem strong ones; and his important discussion of two papyrus fragments on pp. 243f. does not affect this particular question.)

The lost passage must have been quite long, to accommodate laments over several separate limbs and the necessary transitions; longer than 29 verses on the evidence of the papyri just mentioned, perhaps about 50 verses if, as seems possible, the loss was caused by the tearing away of the outer column of a two-column page. Whatever its nature, the accident happened later than the compilation of the *Christus Patiens*—a curious poem on the passion of Christ, which was botched together in the twelfth century A.D. from a manuscript containing the standard selection of Euripidean plays—since the Byzantine work clearly made use of parts of the lost passage. The most important apparently consecutive section that it preserves is as follows:

> Come, old man, the head of the thrice-wretched one
> let us fit on correctly, and reconstruct the whole
> body as harmoniously as we may.
> O dearest face, O youthful cheeks,
> behold, with this covering I hide your head;
> and the bloodstained and furrowed
> limbs. . . .
>
> (*Christus Patiens* 1466ff.)

Most, perhaps all, of this is from *The Bacchae*, but even so we only possess mere scraps of the whole missing scene. Its general outline is clear, but any attempt at detailed reconstruction is out of the question.

1301   After the (lost) laments and reconstitution of the body, AGAUE asks how PENTHEUS was to blame—whether he was infected by her kind of madness.

131

CADMUS *He turned out like all of you, and failed to rev-*
    erence the god.
Therefore the god linked all together into a single fault,
all of you and Pentheus here, so that he destroyed the house—
including me, who, with no male children of my own,   1305
see this offshoot of your womb, unhappy woman,
most shamefully and evilly done to death.
Through him the house saw the light again—it was you, child,
    who held together
my royal palace, being my daughter's son,
and were a terror to the land. No one was willing   1310
to insult the old man, when he saw your
presence; for he would get the punishment he deserved.
But now I shall be an exile, dishonoured, from my home,
the great Cadmus, who sowed the race of Thebans
and reaped the fairest of harvests.   1315
Most beloved of men—for, though you live no longer, still
you shall be counted, child, among those I love most—
no longer will you touch this beard with your hand

1310– Respect for and protection of the old were traditional Greek
1312   virtues, but CADMUS' description of PENTHEUS as *a terror to the
      land* reveals that in this respect too PENTHEUS had an "excess
      of royal disposition" (671). So also 1320–22 disclose an almost
      morbid desire to seek out offenders.

1315   *the fairest of harvests*: both because most harvests are of grain
      whereas this was of men, and because Thebans were renowned
      for their martial qualities.

1316– There is an exaggerated pathos about this description of
1322   PENTHEUS' tenderness that seems characteristic of the literary
      genre of dirges (and was founded, no doubt, on a tradition of
      mourning different from and warmer than our own). It is seen,
      for example, in the laments of Andromache and Hecuba in
      Euripides' *The Trojan Women* (e.g., 634–83, 740–79, 1167–
      1202), and one of its main archetypes is the almost overdrawn
      poignancy of Andromache imagining Astyanax begging for
      scraps in *The Iliad*, 22. 492–501.

and fold me in your arms, calling me "mother's father,"
and saying, "Who is doing you a wrong, old man, or not paying
    due respect?   1320
Who disturbs your heart by being disagreeable to you?
Tell me, so that I may punish the one who wrongs you, grand-
    father."
But now I am utterly wretched, you are miserable indeed,
your mother is an object of pity, your kin are in misery.
If there is any man who despises deity   1325
let him look on Pentheus' death, and judge that gods exist!

    CHORUS   Your fate I grieve for, Cadmus; but your grand-
      child
has a punishment that is deserved, though grievous to you.

    AGAUE   Father, since you see how my fortunes have utterly
    changed

    ·   ·   ·   ·   ·   ·

[A passage is missing here; in the course of it DIONYSUS appears,
in his fully divine form, on the palace roof.]

1323   *miserable indeed*: literally, simply "miserable," just as in the
     next verse; in the catalogue of woe little distinction is drawn
     between the exiled and the dismembered.

1325f Similar things are said about divinely caused disasters in other
     tragedies; what gives CADMUS' declaration a special force is its
     manifestly heartfelt tone in contrast to his specious enthusiasm
     for the god earlier in the play.

1329f It is impossible to tell how AGAUE's utterance was completed
     or how long it was—except that the addition of only a single
     verse might not have provided a sufficiently dramatic occasion
     for DIONYSUS' epiphany.

     The god appears on top of the building at the back of the
    stage, a position reserved for the presentation of gods in their
    own person. Euripides was particularly devoted to the *deus ex
    machina*, the deity who appears at the end of a tragedy (occa-
    sionally suspended from the "machine," a sort of crane, which
    accounts for the Latin expression) to terminate the action and

Dionysus . . . .
you shall be turned into a serpent, and your wife   1330

---

announce the fortunes of the survivors. This was not, of course, due to dramaturgical inadequacy, an inability to resolve the action in any other way, but rather to the fact that the underlying myth usually *did* give the ultimate decision to a god, and Euripides was curiously faithful to certain aspects of the myth. Of course he developed the device for his own special purposes, and particularly, in plays like *Hippolytus* or *Ion*, to give additional complexity to the ambiguous role of the god or goddess; so too with Dionysus here.

1330ff This detailed, and to the modern reader very curious, statement of the future fortunes of the surviving characters is an extreme example of a common device in Euripides, who connected the outcome of many of his plays with known cults, rituals, or practices. Thus in *Medea* the heroine announces the establishment of Corinthian rites in honour of her slain children; in *Hippolytus* Artemis tells the dying hero of a cult to be established in his memory at Trozen; at the end of *Ion* Athena prophesies the ethnic role of Ion's children, and at the end of *Iphigenia in Tauris*, another late play, she gives instructions for founding a cult of Artemis at Halae and Brauron. Not all the rituals were connected with Athens, so an appeal to local patriotism and antiquarianism was not the overriding motive. Rather Euripides seems to have been responding to a common aetiological taste that was particularly marked in the later fifth century B.C. (note on 102–04) and had been accentuated both by the sophists and by the growth of local history (note on 13–19).

It was universally believed that Thebes fell to the sons of the Seven against Thebes immortalized by Aeschylus' play of that name, and Herodotus (5. 61) has a story that the Thebans were then driven out and joined a tribe called the Encheleis, literally "Eels," in Illyria (the modern Montenegro). Furthermore there was evidently a well-known oracle put out by Delphi that barbarians would ravage Apollo's sanctuary there

134

shall change into the savage form of a snake—
Harmonia, daughter of Ares, whom you won though yourself a
    mortal.
With your wife, as the oracle of Zeus declares,
you shall drive an ox-cart, leading foreigners.
Many are the cities you shall overthrow with your numberless   1335
horde; but when they have ravaged the oracle
of Loxias, a miserable return home
shall be theirs; but Ares will rescue you and Harmonia
and transplant your life to the land of the blessed.

---

but afterwards be destroyed; Herodotus (9. 42f.) reports that
this was believed by the Persians, when they invaded Greece,
to refer to themselves, but that actually it referred to the
Encheleis centuries before. Then there is a story known only
from a Byzantine source to the effect that CADMUS, driving
oxen, founded a town in Illyria called Bouthoe, literally
"swift-ox"—a story no doubt based on the much earlier account of his following a cow to the site of Thebes itself. From
this confusion of legends, or something like it, Euripides compounded his own syncretistic account; but why the oddest
detail of all, that CADMUS and his wife Harmonia are to be
turned into snakes? Possibly it reflects one form in which
CADMUS had long ago been worshipped in Thebes, as the house-
or palace-snake, the genius and protector of the place (note on
102–04). That, combined with the association of the Cadmeians with the "Eels," may somehow have accounted for this
part of the story. It is unlikely that Euripides himself invented
it, and he certainly did not invent the final detail, that CAD-
MUS and Harmonia would eventually go to the Isles of the
Blessed; for Pindar, for example, had placed CADMUS there
(Olympians 2. 78), no doubt because he was married to Harmonia, who was divine through her father Ares (1338, 1357)
in his union with Aphrodite. CADMUS had offended Ares when
he founded Thebes, by killing the dragon that guarded Ares'
spring; he expiated the offence, was given Ares' daughter in
marriage, and had all the gods to his wedding.

1337   Loxias is a name for Apollo.

135

All this I say as offspring of no mortal father   1340
but of Zeus—I, Dionysus. If you had recognized
how to behave sanely, when you refused to, you would have had
the son of Zeus as ally, and would now be happy.

> CADMUS   *Dionysus, we beseech you! We have done wrong!*

> DIONYSUS   *You were late to understand us. When you*
> *should have, you did not know us.*   1345

> CADMUS   *This we have come to recognize; but your reprisals*
> *are too severe!*

> DIONYSUS   *Yes, because I am a god, and you insulted me.*

> CADMUS   *Gods should not resemble men in their anger!*

> DIONYSUS   *Long ago Zeus my father approved these things.*

1345   *You were late to understand us:* a persistent note in and before
Greek tragedy, a modulation of the proverb "by suffering,
learning" (*pathei mathos*) stressed by Aeschylus in his *Agamemnon* (177): if you do not understand the gods *now* you
will learn about them the hard way. The frank admission of
wrongdoing, as by CADMUS in 1344, is no excuse and will not
remit a fraction of the suffering that has been earned.

1347– DIONYSUS implies that no punishment can be too great for
1349   insulting a god; and indeed this was a common view among
men, and the CHORUS, too, had insisted that the proper punishment for impiety is death (1002–4). Yet CADMUS correctly
recognizes a tone of wounded *amour-propre*, and suggests that
gods should be above this. DIONYSUS' reply, which seems to
silence him, is that the outcome was approved by Zeus long
ago—a reply that has struck modern critics as intolerably weak,
or perhaps as a deliberate piece of hostile characterization by
the poet (p. 8). But, as Dodds observes, there are several
other Euripidean contexts where a deity defends his actions by
invoking higher authority; and I doubt whether any special
significance should be read into this verse or whether it should
be used to indicate Euripides' own opinion of the god.

AGAUE   Alas, the decision is made, old man: a miserable
    exile.   1350

DIONYSUS   Why then delay over what is inevitable?

CADMUS   My child, how terrible the evil we have come to,
all of us—you and your sisters
and my wretched self! I shall arrive among foreigners
as an aged and alien settler; and there still remains for me the
    divine decree   1355
of leading into Hellas a motley, barbarian horde.
And Ares' child Harmonia, my wife,
I shall lead against the altars and tombs of the Hellenes
in the savage form of a serpent—I a serpent too,
and leader of the spearsmen; nor shall I have respite   1360

1352–   The play ends in repetitious lamentations and expressions of
1392   self-pity. Little new is said, and the poetical level is unremark-
        able. Some critics have thought, therefore, that the ending,
        notably the anapestic part (see note on 1368–92), has been
        expanded or reworked by someone other than Euripides. Yet
        Greek tragedies regularly close with a relaxation of tension.
        Here the climax was reached first with PENTHEUS' death and
        then with AGAUE's self-recognition; after that it is important
        that the fate of those who opposed the god should be relent-
        lessly made known both to them and to the audience. All the
        same, the hackneyed quality of 1372–80 comes as something
        of a surprise; Euripides can be automatic, but *The Bacchae*
        in general is remarkably fresh and underivative. It is also a
        fact that the endings of plays were particularly liable to altera-
        tion.

1360–   CADMUS' implied complaint about going to the Isles of the
1362   Blessed would strike the audience as unnatural—"at peace"
        is just what the fortunate ones who went there were, whereas
        sailing down the river Acheron led to the troubled half-life of
        the ordinary dead in Hades. The exaggerated pathos of dirges
        (note on 1316–22) may be a factor; if not, there is some im-
        plication that he is being unduly fussy. That would entail a

137

from troubles, wretched that I am, nor down precipitous
Acheron shall I sail and come to be at peace.

AGAUE (embracing CADMUS)   O father, I shall be exiled
   and parted from you!

CADMUS   Why do you throw your arms around me, unhappy
   child,
as the swan protects its white-plumed drone of a parent?   1365

AGAUE   For where shall I turn, an outcast from this land?

CADMUS   I do not know, child. Your father is a poor helper.

AGAUE   Farewell, palace, farewell, land
             of my fathers. In misfortune I leave you,
             a fugitive from my own home.   1370

CADMUS   Go, then, child, to Aristaeus'

                .   .   .   .   .   .

             [probably a single verse missing here]

---

momentary reminder of his rather absurd character at the
beginning of the play. Apart from these words, CADMUS is
consistently shown at the play's end as sensible and dignified.

1365   *white-plumed*: suggests grey old age as well as the ordinary
       colour of the swan; *drone*, too, stresses age, because of the
       inability to work. The elements of the comparison were
       familiar in poetry, but their use here is not completely suc-
       cessful either in expression or in application (swans were
       renowned for protecting their parents, but AGAUE's gesture
       is an appeal for help)—unless we are to see a cynical reflec-
       tion by the poet on the self-centredness both of AGAUE and
       of her father at this point.

1368– The metre changes to a marching rhythm based on the
1392   anapaest, $\cup \cup -$, for which the dactyl, $- \cup \cup$, can often be
       substituted.

1371   In view of what he had said at 1367, CADMUS is unlikely to
       be naming a place of refuge for AGAUE and her sisters *outside*

AGAUE	*I mourn for you, father.*
CADMUS	*And I for you, child,* *and I weep for your sisters.*
AGAUE	*For terribly has lord* *Dionysus brought this outrage* 1375 *upon your house.*
CADMUS	*Yes, because he was terribly treated by you,* *and his name went without honour in Thebes!*
AGAUE	*Farewell, father.*
CADMUS	*Farewell, my pitiable* *daughter, fare well—though this would be* *hard for you to attain!* 1380

Thebes—even though, according to a later account, Aristaeus (Actaeon's father; note on 1227f.) had left Thebes at his son's death. So presumably CADMUS is simply telling AGAUE to go to Aristaeus' (and therefore Autonoe's) house in the city, to collect her sisters (1381f.).

1377f With several other critics I assume a minute corruption of a single letter in the verb termination. The sole manuscript gives *epaschon*, "I suffered," which means that the speaker must be DIONYSUS and that he has been kept onstage in silence and for some time (since 1351) just to make this not very pointed statement. If the correct reading is *epaschen*, "he suffered," as is assumed in the translation, then the speaker is CADMUS and the god can have departed after 1351—itself not a very strong cue, but a possible one. Lines 1377f. come quite naturally from CADMUS (and are interesting since they make him emphasize more strongly than elsewhere that the guilt was AGAUE's and her sisters' rather than his own), and they give a more balanced and continuous exchange of speakers.

1380 This is CADMUS' final utterance, but it is doubtful whether he leaves the stage at this point. His daughter has been saying goodbye to him, rather than vice versa; she certainly turns

AGAUE (turning offstage)   *Lead me, you friends who send me*
forth, to where we shall collect
my sisters as pitiable companions in exile.
May I come where
neither dire Cithaeron may see me,
nor my eyes see Cithaeron,   1385
nor where is any thyrsus dedicated, to remind
me!
Let these be the concern of other bac-
chants.

CHORUS   *Many are the shapes of things divine;*
much the gods achieve beyond expectation;
and what seems probable is not accomplished,   1390
whereas for the improbable, god finds a way.
Such was the result of this affair.

---

away, and the question will arise whether *she* will leave the
stage after 1387—or whether both she and CADMUS are envisaged as proceeding out with the CHORUS. The point is
doubtful, and I have inserted no stage directions in the text.

1383– After the conventional lamentations that have preceded, these
1387 words of utter disillusionment seem even more striking: AGAUE
is disgusted with Cithaeron, and Cithaeron with her. She does
not claim that thyrsi should no longer be dedicated (i.e., that
the worship of DIONYSUS should not continue), but simply
that she personally cannot bear to think of them.

1388– A coda such as this, sung in marching rhythm as the CHORUS
1392 walk in procession out of the orchestra, was conventional for
Sophocles and Euripides. Indeed this very one occurs in four
other Euripidean plays (though slightly modified in *Medea*),
all of them containing a strong reversal of fortune. Other plays,
for example, have a prayer for victory in its place. The present
coda is beautifully appropriate here, and it echoes themes
sounded by the CHORUS already in the Third Stasimon (888f.,
906–9); its formal yet familiar quality stresses the ritualistic
origins of the drama, the inevitability of the human predica-
ment, and the inscrutable power of the gods.

BIBLIOGRAPHY

EDITIONS

Dodds, E. R., ed., *Euripides: Bacchae*, 2nd ed. Oxford: Clarendon Press, 1960.
Roux, Jeanne, *Euripide, les Bacchantes*, 2 vols. Paris: Les Belles Lettres 1970–2

CRITICISM

Conacher, D. J., *Euripidean Drama: Myth, Theme and Structure*. Toronto: University of Toronto Press, 1967.
Grube, G. M. A., *The Drama of Euripides*, 2nd ed. London: Methuen, 1961.
Lucas, Donald W., *The Greek Tragic Poets*. New York: W. W. Norton & Company, Inc., 1964.
Murray, Gilbert, *Euripides and His Age*, 2nd ed. London: Oxford University Press, 1965.
Segal, Erich, ed., *Euripides: A Collection of Critical Essays*. Englewood Cliffs, N. J.: Prentice-Hall, Inc., 1968.
Webster, T. B. L., *The Tragedies of Euripides*. London: Methuen, 1967.
Winnington-Ingram, R. P., *Euripides and Dionysus*. Cambridge: Cambridge University Press, 1948.

TRANSLATIONS

Arrowsmith, W., in *The Complete Greek Tragedies*, Vol. 5, eds. D. Green and R. Lattimore. Chicago: University of Chicago Press, 1959.
Vellacott, P., *Euripides: Three Plays*. Harmondsworth, Middlesex, England: Penguin Books, Ltd., 1953.

141